SoZoKi

Creation's Energy

We know from our earliest science lessons that everything is made of atoms which consist of protons, electrons, and neutrons. What wasn't made clear was that everything is energy. And not only every thing but also all of life. Everything about people – from our thoughts and feelings to our laughter and dreams – is energy.

To provide a handle with which to discuss this incredible energy, I have created the word *SoZoKi* from two Japanese words: *Sozo* translates to Creation and *Ki* to Energy, and together mean Creation Energy. SoZoki is the Creation Energy that all of life is about.

Read on for the exciting details about how SoZoKi can change your life. Oh, and as you are going to want to tell your friends about SoZoKi, you should know how to pronounce it. *So* and *Zo* as they are spelled and *Ki* like *key,* with equal emphasis on each syllable.

SoZoKi

Creation's Energy

SoZoKi
Creation's Energy

by Nancy Anna Blitz

Charlottesville, Virginia
Carmel, California

June 2021

First Edition

This is a work of historical fiction, based almost entirely on facts extracted from tireless research. There is a soupçon of creative license exercised in these pages, but nothing that alters the tone and truth of what happened during this extraordinary time as recounted here.

SoZoKi
Creation's Energy

Table of Contents

Publisher's Note

When I moved from concrete canyons of New York City to the redwood canyons Mill Valley in "marvy" Marin County just north of the Golden Gate Bridge, it didn't take long to realize that I was in a different world. Hot tubs, peacock feathers, and all sorts of new ideas and even language. I'm sure that I had heard about meditating though I hadn't practiced it, but chakras were not in my vocabulary. And energy, if it wasn't about fossil fuels, was the vim and vigor I hoped to be able to summon when needed.

I met a lot of interesting people who lived different lives and who were willing to share their knowledge; and to do so with the requisite patience in dealing with someone who at thirty already pretty much knew everything. Over the next couple of years, with my certainty upended by Life's different plan, I listened with greater interest and poked significant gaps in my cocksureness.

Over forty years, those holes have morphed into sinkholes, sending much of what I thought I knew crumbling into history. Rising from the rubble has been a greater awareness of, and curiosity about, synchronicity and the Energy that is the source of everything.

A good thing, too, because when I received this manuscript, I could not only understand what Nancy Anna Blitz had written, but it validated some key issues that I had been exploring.

Why you should read this book – what is so special about it – is the author. Nancy explains what is the true path to good health. She does it from the perspective of significant hands-on work in Western medicine and with Eastern energy systems. Her credentials are impressive. She was in scrubs for several decades, many of those years as an operating room nurse. She also applied herself to deep studies of several non-medical ways of healing, including becoming a Reiki Master.

To our benefit, she reports key aspects of what she has learned in readable and comprehensible detail, so that we too can live healthier and more rewarding lives.

Tony Seton
Carmel, California

Editor's Note

I first met Nancy Blitz at a night club, both of us there for the love of live music. Once you meet Nancy you can't forget her, and once you get to know her you'll never doubt her generosity, or her passion for helping and healing others. Or, for that matter, her enthusiasm for concerts. In the quieter moments between tunes I learned that she was working on a book, a spiritual manual that could be used to teach nurses to tap into their own creative, healing energies through an Eastern-derived practice she had named "SoZoKi." When I told her I did editing work our collaborative partnership was born.

Nancy began writing many of the chapters that eventually became this book during a period of wandering in the spiritual desert, wondering if she should change course completely and leave nursing for good. Instead, she burrowed into her cozy house and with her two little dogs for company she listened, questioned and meditated, and The Soul's

Path (title of original manuscript) began to take shape. And then it rushed into being, and chapter by chapter she emailed me the book as it emerged. Nancy poured her life experiences into words she hoped would guide others to the insights she'd received through her travels, her trials, her years mastering the unforgiving environment of the modern medical operating theater and later the disciplines of nurse management and hospital administration. I wonder if she knew when she began to write just how much she had to say, how richly the tapestry of her own life illustrated the stories that interweave all our human lives.

All that abundance engendered its own problems, of course. What to leave in? What to leave out? Most of all, how to quicken the interest of the reader and then engage, explain and teach, step-by-step, her SoZoKi practice? We struggled at times over these questions but Nancy's passion never flagged. Never faltered. Like the crystals she uses to align ethereal energy she used the manuscript to align her story, and to bring her knowledge into a form others could access on their own.

So The Soul's Path might best be understood as a gift, to the healers who care for the sick and injured, to any one soul seeking to rejoin the creative, loving energy that surrounds us, if we can but pause and allow it to flow freely through ourselves, in and out like our breath, healing and whole.

It's been a wonderful journey working on this book. I've learned much from Nancy's unstoppable energy, her cheerful determination and her passion to serve. I hope I have helped to shape the book so that it will help to shape, as she intends, the lives it touches. And in the quieter moments between songs, I look forward to congratulating her on keeping the faith that SoZoKi practice can change our worlds.

Annie Becker
Charlottesville, Virginia
January 2021

Author's Note

There is a multitude of opportunities that help us focus on our spirit's energy. Religion has been utilized for millennia to bring or force – depending on when in history and your individual perspective – human consciousness to entertain ethereal concepts meant to help humanity's spirit through this Earth-grounding experience. Angels and saints, shamans and mystics, crosses and stars, traditions and rituals...all have survived to keep us on the righteous path toward the next level of ascension. Meditation practices, yoga, chakras, moon cycles, smudging, and incense, while considered new age, are heavily rooted in ancient traditions to connect to spirit. Tribal and religious leaders around the globe continue to teach ancient practices to heal the body and guide the mind to spirit energy. All approaches find themselves somewhere along the path of evolving our human consciousness to our spirit's consciousness.

Yet it is easy to get caught up in the negative

thoughts of human failure. When we look around our world and observe the vast amount of behavior that continues to harm, control, or eradicate, and that is all we allow ourselves to see, our view negates the actual progress we have made. If we broaden our view as we look back through the recorded history of humanity, we can most certainly see that human consciousness has evolved, albeit in different ways in different societies. While there are still wars being fought, there are also many organizations and enterprises, both secular and faith-based, working to help peoples around our world regardless of nationality, race, or creed. These humans helping other humans in need is a significant step up from people only helping those who share the same belief system or are members of the same clan or tribe. This offers clear proof that our human consciousness has and continues to evolve.

How does this evolution still allow for the individual caught up in one belief system? Why are there still those who believe their way is the only way to return to what is most often identified as 'God'? Why are there still faith-based charities that limit their help to only those who convert to their belief system? Why are religions still causing so much division with many the root cause of war, death, and destruction? We are not evolved, we are evolving, we are a work in progress and each of us contributes to raising our human to our spirit's consciousness. A promise of utopia, not hardly, for we would still be subject to natural elements, the laws of nature negatively impacting our experience, but humanity would not be the cause.

Ésprit SoZoKi – a lively spirit with Creation's Energy – is an opportunity to learn and practice the art of bringing wellness-enhancing energy into your everyday life. So just in case you are giving an arch look at this book, thinking that I might be planning to establish the next great religion, please relax. That's the farthest thing from my mind. This isn't a new group plan. It's instead providing a healthy and liberating map for you to chart your personal well-being, so that you can see and feel the proof of your own individual evolution to greater understanding of the hows and whys of the life you are living. And most importantly, to provide you with the tools to feel better in body and soul.

Nancy Anna Blitz

Dedication

To my son,

Tyler Mosely Blitz Ruff

To my parents,

Jenelle Malloy Blitz

Victor Edward Blitz

&

You now reading

May you paint the most beautiful portrait

of your holy spirit for humanity.

Introduction

Everything we see, touch, smell, hear, and taste, is energy that has condensed to physical form so that spirit, our soul, can have this human experience. Understand that the energy I speak of is not based on some particular scientific theory, nor is it the foundation for a religious doctrine. Simply stated, it is the energy that is found in everything, be it animate or inanimate. All that we sense, every thought and feeling we experience, is energy. It is energy in the form of gravity that holds us to the Earth. In another form, we see large energy weather systems propelling damaging storms through the sky. But it is also energy that defines the beauty of the sun's rise and set. This omnipresent energy is not just here on this planet; it takes form everywhere from our solar system and throughout the universe to all that exists. From before the Big Bang to forever infinity in all directions of time and space, never ending.

Many minds are challenged to comprehend everywhere and forever. Others may associate this energy with an *Omnipotent God* source. It is my experience it is accessible to everyone, regardless of any religious or philosophical belief; even to those numerologists whose calculations are said to dispute the existence of God.

Openness to the unknown is the first step to acceptance of all purposeful paths in life. Awareness to what is possible ignites our ability to create and examine structured thinking. Yes, it takes thought, which I would remind you is energy, and that thought/energy leads you forward to greater knowledge and understanding in a new way.

As noted on the first page, I came up with a new word to identify and describe this amazing energy. I put together two Japanese words; *Sozo*, which means Creation and *Ki* which is Energy. SoZoki is the Creation Energy that embodies everything, providing a concrete view of what we call life.

But this book is not a gimmick or an idle pitch, based on scientific studies. In truth, it illustrates how my personal experiences helped me recognize the ways that Creation Energy functions in our everyday lives. And best of all, how anyone can use it to create healthier bodies and minds. There is no trade-off, there is no cost. As you will discover in these pages, SoZoKi is a liberating experience that gives you quality control over your life.

Dispersed throughout this book is a QRcode. Use the camera on your smart phone to access www.SoZoKi.com to learn more about Éspirit with SoZoKi.

<u>*1 - When I* Get *I'll* Be</u>

This chapter is a brief, introductory review of patterns of human behavior and history from antiquity to the 21st century. We have traversed a path through millennia, down through the generations, from spirit-based traditions and beliefs to acquisitive, secular materialism, followed by a return, at least in the West, to spiritualism. I hope to show the continuity of this evolution. Finally, in the closing section I attempt to open the reader's mind, and spark the imagination, by offering for contemplation and consideration ancient questions which may never fully be answered.

<u>Spirit to Secular</u>

I am a nurse and a healer, not a historian, but I do believe we need to pay attention to the history of ideas and ideals ever evolving within the human story. In this book I endeavor to paint that history with a broad brush, touching on a few of the many great thinkers who have propelled that evolution, seeing them as representative of larger trends and in some cases serving as catalysts for fundamental, historic change.

Historical recounting also reveals the development of our spiritual awareness and documents the human tendency to swing from one extreme of belief to another, moving forward only to fall back. Millennia after millennia, we witness failures of religious or civil authorities to act in the best interests of the people they lead, committing in some cases crimes against the very humanity they purport to serve. We witness this now, in the 21st century. And we witness the pendulum swinging the other way as well, as societies flourish and human potential blossoms.

Across religions and cultures we see mirrored practices that repeat, though the faces change. Radicalized subsects of Islam call their followers to Holy War; Evangelical Christians vehemently condemn to Hell souls who decline to accept Jesus Christ as their sole and necessary Savior. Both sects are inciting war, on both the human psyche and on the Holy Spirit itself as representative of our better nature, our Holy Spirit. No soul is bad. But cruelty amongst individuals or the mass cruelty of war will continue until we take responsibility ourselves for our choices, their impact on humanity and education of spirit consciousness, for our evolution. There remains hope for the spirit, as will be seen when we examine the historical record.

Looking back, then, we see the Middle Ages which followed the Fall of the Roman Empire, when many of the beneficial insights and advances of Classical Antiquity were lost. The Pax Romana (27 BC to 180 AD), which had imposed peace on Europe and fostered exchanges of ideas between nations, gave way to a time relatively devoid of intellectual activity. Evidence exists of great human migrations during this 1,000-year period, yet artistic and cultural pursuits languished. Economies shrank, knowledge and skills were lost, and cultural pursuits gave way to a grim, subsistence life.

The Renaissance Era, beginning in the 1400s, saw a rebirth of art, philosophy, and social progress. The chaos that had endured for centuries gave way to new exploration of the gifts of Antiquity that had been lost. Ideals are the full, perfect flowering of ideas, and Western civilization moved from utilitarian dominance and brute existence to scholasticism (dogma and beliefs relating to politics, religion, and philosophy) and then to humanism (man as the measure of all things).

Exploration of the physical world's geography and the natural laws that it seemingly must obey laid a foundation for a new kind of human understanding. Sometimes referred to as the Age of Enlightenment, this exploration was not originally secular in intent, but as the mechanisms of nature began to be revealed, new ways to describe and appreciate phenomena arose. The rushing sound of wind across a plain no longer needed be described as the voice of spirits good or evil. It was instead possible to perceive the natural, reproducible result of atmosphere interacting with landscape. The intention to explore the meaning of life was eclipsed by the pursuit to understand the material nature of the universe.

Thomas Paine, an English political activist, theorist, revolutionary and philosopher, arrived in the Thirteen Colonies of the New World just in time to embroil himself in the American Revolution. He published an influential pamphlet in 1776. Entitled *Common Sense*, it crystallized the popular colonial demand for freedom from Great Britain. John Adams, second president of the new United States, later said that "without the pen of the author of *Common Sense*, the sword of [George] Washington would have been raised in vain."

Imprisoned for his beliefs in a French jail in 1794, Paine wrote *The Age of Reason*, in which he professed his belief in one God and hope for happiness beyond this life, while simultaneously rejecting formal religion. He declared that the equality of men transcended nations, as did the duties of practicing mercy and justice and helping others in the search for happiness. Actual communication from God to man was possible, in his view, but once the revelation was shared it became "second-hand knowledge," no longer sacred.

During the century following Paine's death, a German philosopher named Georg Wilhelm Friedrich Hegel proposed the concept of absolute realism, the idea being that in order to be able to reason, humans must possess some sense of identity of thought and being, that is conscious of and comprehends the world around us. This line of thought, that things only exist in relation to the self, stimulated the development of atheism, a philosophy rather than a religion, which emphasized the role of intellect in our perceptions of humanity and deity. Hegel's thinking influenced Karl Marx and Friedrich Engels, as well as Friedrich Wilhelm Nietzsche.

Europe was rocked by social upheaval during this period. Aristocracies were violently overthrown by the masses, the people whose lives were controlled at every step by a system of birthright order in which basic human rights were subject to the whims and favor of a tiny class of nobility. Wealth and power were concentrated in this ruling class; human development was effectively crushed and cultural growth stifled. Economies stagnated. Marx and Engels identified revolutionary violence as an inevitable result of capitalist practice, itself a consequence of social changes brought about by the Industrial Revolution. Their *Communist Manifesto* bore witness to the abuses of child labor and exploitation of adults as profits flowed and overflowed to the owner's pocketbooks. Empowered by production, the factories poisoned the very breath of the Continent.

The early ideals of communism lay in organizing communes filled with working people who earned their livelihoods and improved their earthly lot through cooperative action, rather than under the fist of a strong central government or small ruling class. Communism itself was not anti-religion at first, but later thinkers brought their own tragic experiences to bear, suggesting that God did not care, after all, for humanity, or possibly did not even exist. For many the belief that life should be lived to the betterment of human experience in the here and now replaced centuries of religious dogma that offered up human suffering in this life for a better life in God's presence after death.

Influenced by the ancient Indian and Egyptian beliefs of eternal rebirth, as well as the radical social philosophies of his time, Friedrich Wilhelm Nietzsche wrote *Thus Spoke Zarathustra,* a novel expanding on his theory that experience and energy recur infinitely across time and space. The book inspired one of the most notable composers of the day, Gustav Mahler, to write his famous Symphony No. 3. When Nietzsche observed the effect of Mahler's music on the suffering lower classes, lifting their spirits from despair to joy, his convictions regarding man and religion were confirmed. He wrote

Beyond Good and Evil to further expose what he called "slave morality," the Christian teaching that humility and meekness in the face of poverty and suffering are redeeming and lead to eternal abundance and peace in the afterlife. Nietzsche believed this line of thought kept society in a state of mediocrity and inhibited the realization of great human potential. He rejected the notion that well-being should not be sought after by ordinary people in their own lifetimes.

Up until that time it was widely believed in Europe that only the clergy of the established Church were privileged to have the ear of God, which kindled widespread corruption. Among that corruption was the practice of placing a monetary price on intervention on behalf of parishioners.

Change came by the dawn of the modern era; God and clergy were no longer the sole heirs to knowledge and social control. In the early part of the 20th century Adolf Hitler exploited the absence of a dominant religious ethic by rallying Germans, and others, instead around nationalist politics and doctrines of racial purity. Nietzsche's ideal of the realized individual, the Superman, was twisted into a doctrine of racial superiority. The redeeming social values of the Church gave way to a demonizing of outsiders, and Jews became the scapegoats in a Europe that was struggling to recover from the devastation of the First World War. Ordinary citi-

zens accepted increasingly violent policies that led
first to the establishment of ghettoes and eventually
to an organized campaign to eradicate not only
Jews but Gypsies and intellectuals, homosexuals
and the disabled, among other "undesirable" seg-
ments of the populace. Mass deportation and death
camps followed. God, it seemed, was dead.

Materialism

The drive to explore the ethereal meaning of life
was eclipsed by the pursuit to understand the material nature of the universe. Having turned from
mysticism and religious ideology, Western thought
was redirected towards the pursuit of happiness in
the present, tangible world. The acquisition of
wealth and influence, even power, became an end
in itself. And so was born our present-day dilemma,
"When I get, then I'll be," only to become disenchanted and identify the next in a never-ending
pursuit of happiness evidenced by possession.
"Keeping up with the Joneses," the idea that to have
value one must possess at least as much as, if not
more than, our fellows. Purposeful relentless pursuit to possess, actions, things, or people, is an ex-
emplary example of human consciousness overpowering the spirit. Hence, spirit consciousness
circles the drain of acquisition.

Although it is sometimes said that wealth is the root

of all evil, implying that those who seek it are on the wrong path, it is rather when the desire for material gain becomes the central focus of one's life, when the welfare of others becomes secondary to the acquisition of wealth, that problems arise. The pursuit of earthly gains can bring forth opportunities to elevate one's own spirituality and raise up others, but when the end goal is domination and exploitation, the result is the deprivation, starvation, and degradation of societies that has poisoned our collective history and persists to this very day.

Pax Romana	27BC - 180CE	Antiquity
Middle Ages	5th C - 15th C	Mass Migrations
Renaissance	1400	Reawakening
Thomas Paine	1776 - 1794	*Common Sense* *Age of Reason*
Hegel	1770 - 1831 1818 - 1883	Absolute Realism
Marx & Engels	1820 -1895	Communism
Nietzsche	1844 - 1900	*Slave Morality* Realized Individualism
Hitler	1889 - 1945	Supreme Race
Nancy	1956 - TBD	SoZoKi

2 - *Perception and Life Experiences*

Perception is sensory awareness in the presence of stimuli that serves to assist understanding, recognition, envisioning, or discerning an experience. Influenced by parental training, genetic inheritance, personal experience, and subconscious influences, accepting and rejecting conventional wisdom is more than an isolated individual process. Through societal norms, belief systems, and common expectations of acceptable behavior, perception pervades decision-making with consequences across the human continuum. Have you ever wondered why so often, in the face of factual evidence, our personal experiences and subjective perception nonetheless determine the decisions we make in life? This can be on a micro or macro scale. While decisions may impact an individual life, they can also impact a society, even an entire race, and the outcome can elevate or damn human beings.

Parental Domestication

To domesticate is take something unfamiliar and make it more ordinary, familiar, and acceptable. Humans have domesticated animals for centuries, taking from Nature the familiar animals we now call pets and livestock. Generations of breeding changed wild to tame, sometimes even demure or docile. Theories on human self-domestication have been researched and genetic evidence is gaining ground for the understanding that human selection of companions was based on pro-social behaviors, that is to say, we domesticated ourselves.

When we raise our children, very early we begin to teach them about life. It starts with meeting their needs for comfort, food, and security. When they cry, we respond, shaping their expectations, regardless of whether our responses nurture or neglect. This process is the same for most if not all children and influences their perceptions of reality throughout their lives.

Feral children have been found in multiple sites around the world. Often abandoned by parents with alcohol and/or drug addictions, they have been isolated from human society for prolonged periods of time in early childhood. Once discovered, these children have social and intellectual deficits they cannot overcome despite all efforts. They often take on the characteristics of wild animals – often those of canines but occasionally primates – they have lived with to survive.

Street urchins, children raising themselves in the streets of slums, face many of the intellectual challenges of the feral child. Often shunned as dirty and mischievous, their behaviors are the result of the daily struggle for survival, and their appearances reflect that struggle. Without the benefit of parental domestication, these children grow into adults with psycho-social deficits, repeatedly failing to meet their own basic needs, and depending on society to do for them, frequently in mental health or penal institutions. These children may grow into adults who mistrust authority as well as charitable organizations. In some cases developing trust takes a lifetime. Their perception of the world is as a cruel place filled with intention to harm. Had they been given the same opportunities as a child raised in a loving family the outcome could have been far different.

I was raised with ideas imprinted upon me by both my mother and father, as many of us are. My mother's refrain, "Can't never could, Nancy", was invoked every time I started to give up on an idea or action. I remind myself of her statement every time I think I'll quit a project before completion, and I continue to make the effort required to accomplish a goal I set. I can't recall the number of times her words rang in my ears as I worked on my Master's degree or as I work on drawing a portrait.

People first viewing a piece of my artwork often think it as photo. Only because I stay the course am I able to finish a portrait so detailed that it fools the eye and is worthy of their surprise and admiration when I share that it is actually a drawing.

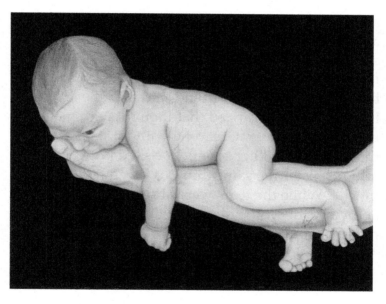

"In One Hand" (2006)

Drawing by Nancy Anna Blitz

My mother also taught me that external beauty is a genetic gift, but far more important is the beauty within a person. To this day I observe beautiful countenances rapidly turn ugly as they express inner meanness, and I hold my mother's truth in the center of my heart and mind today.

I wrote the poem "Nanny" for her 2010 Mother's Day gift, and then read it at her funeral in 2014. My sister, Jane, had shared a story the night before about a friend who had lost a young son and was able to eloquently speak at his funeral, without tears, in a strong, loving voice. Asked how she had been able to do so, her friend said that she loved him that much. I carried that thought with me to my mother's funeral, reading without pause to those who loved her so much. Asked how I did it, I told my sister the same thing, "I loved her that much." While the tears were absent from my face and voice, my heart filled and then overflowed in my final goodbye to my mom.

Nanny

There once was a dame, Jenelle was her name
And she lived in the heart of Dixie
Deep in the south, in her beautiful brick house
Surrounded by Fairies and Pixies
While she could not see, as they played in the leaves
She pondered the length of her life
The roles she had played, as she lived through her days
A mother, a nurse and a wife
Four children she had, with some help from their dad
She raised them to love and to care
They each had a home, and once they were grown
The lessons they learned they did share
With the children they had, now gown past girls and lad
They all knew her as their Nanny
Now she has passed, yet within every heart
Her love resides in each nook and cranny

Nancy Anna Blitz
May 2010 (Mother's Day)
July 18, 2018 (edited edition)

From my father came, "The road to hell is paved with good intentions, Nancy Anna!" each time I attempted to defend myself with, "I didn't mean to". When I heard both my first and middle names coming from him, I knew he meant business and I needed to take heed. He was a strict but loving man and gave me three essential things to remember.

The first is that humans have a strong tendency to push the panic button. Each time he saw me moving in that direction he would say, "Nancy, don't push the panic button; work your way through it!" The second profound gift he gave was, "Keep smiling Nancy. Don't let the bastards get you down!" The third was, "Everything in life is negotiable but your integrity."

I have kept his insights close to my heart and do my best every day to live up to those pearls of wisdom. Those who know me find my father in me today, as I make an honest effort to keep them in my mind and live them in my life. Being able to stop myself from "pushing the panic button" has helped me as an operating room nurse, especially in trauma cases, enabling me to stay focused on those actions required for successful outcomes. Ask any OR nurse and they will tell you, "There is no room for panic in an operating room!"

While resting one evening I heard someone say, "Look, she even smiles in her sleep." But in all honesty, there is not always a smile in my heart. The one lesson I have never broken, though, is that my integrity is not and has never been negotiable.

Daddy-O

This memorial is for you,
The precious father that I knew.
You are no longer here with me,
But in my heart, I do believe
You brought me up to find the place
Where I belong in the human race.
It was a gift that you were given,
to love and teach me to be driven,
And to instill a sense of right in me.
(And honestly, we could agree
It wasn't easy to share your faith --
I still push back at this late date.)
So here I sit and think of you.
A special day, but it's nothing new
That every day you're in my heart
Although your body is no longer part
Of this life's work. That can be hard.
I live to honor your words from afar:
That truth be placed always above self.
To lie is to harm those of us you left.

Daddy-O I still love you so.
Throughout my life, I'll continue to show
That the gift you gave endures in me,
That trust is born from integrity.

And when we trust we can do great things
to fulfill the life that God's grace brings.
So to each and every human being
I wish you love, and hope you sing
In this dance of life, with gratitude
For the little things and the great ones too --
Had my father not lived I would not write
So I thank you, Dad, for giving me life.

June 17, 2017 (rev.) September 19, 2018

My parents were wonderful people and I believe
their intentions were only the best for me and my
siblings, but I recognized early in life they were
products of their own experiences. They carried the
limitations of their generation.

Genetic Inheritance

Generation after generation, DNA has been coding human genetic memory. With each new birth, information is retained and incorporated into the human genome, repeating the pattern over a vast expanse of time. This inherited genetic memory contains common experiences of our species that have been retained through genetic coding. Part of the process has been the identification of beneficial or harmful stimuli, which has refined the ability to survive a plethora of opportunities with the potential to end the existence of the human being on earth. Yet when we take into account choice and free-will, our ability to impact the outcome of an experience, and the multitude of available paths to determine whether that experience has been beneficial or harmful, it can be seen that our behaviors influence genetic inheritance. As we participate in a variety of experiences, is it possible that our genetic inheritance, our ancestral DNA coding, pervades our everyday perceptions and impacts ordinary behavior?

Within each cell exists encoded DNA in the 23 pair of chromosomes which houses the complete set of nucleic acid sequences for humans. Contained in germ cells (the sperm gamete and the egg) are three billion DNA base pairs. That sounds like an enormous amount of information potential, yet each germ cell holds only half of the opportunities which will be found in the somatic cells that give rise to the development of the human embryo, fetus, and then delivered newborn human being.

It is necessary to explore human evolution to make advances in diagnosis and treatment of disease and fulfill expectations of further understanding. The concept of transmission of generational traits, acquired through use or disuse of behaviors during a lifetime, is known as "inheritance of acquired characteristics, or soft inheritance," a hypothesis first conceived in the classical era. This is also known as behavioral traits, and while still questionably recognized, was some of the fundamental work of Darwin. Simply stated in his book *On the Origin of Species*, Darwin recognized the influence of domestication on variation.

Twelve years ago I smoked cigarettes, and I would often find myself holding a lighter in each hand. I didn't intentionally pick them up. I didn't need both of them at the time. Yet, again and again, I would find them in my hands. I recall saying out loud, "Nancy, you don't have to worry about not having a source of fire," and then pondering the importance of man's ability to control fire in the evolution of the human being. Of all available genetic information passed to me from the myriad and multitude of generations that have contributed to my particular life experience as Nancy, having fire has been a recurrent theme. It serves as a reminder that life is far greater than one lifetime, understanding that every lifetime imprints upon humanity all that has been before it.

Over the years I have pondered the idea that God or Creation interacts with a human in a manner or method to which the individual has a capacity. For me, this concept gives voice to the diversity of experience, be it formal or informal, religious faith healing or scientific discoveries, or the yin/yang aspects of transgender identity. Our spirit's journey is not just intentional but purposeful. However, events can influence the perception of the world that surrounds.

Subconscious Influences

Within psychological circles, there is a wide variety of theories addressing subconscious behaviors, as our subconscious mind is responsible for an estimated 99.9% of activity. Limitations on research linger as equipment capable of scientific examination of the subconscious are yet to be developed. This deficit requires we continue seeking knowledge by exploring ideologies with that intent, loosely stated, Freud suggested we store everything at a subconscious level that is pushed into active emotions producing behaviors rather than our conscious intention. Cognitive psychology offers the subconscious as a bundle of cognitive (mental) actions that occur without awareness and are not an independent entity of the mind.

Out of experience, to which our senses are exposed, is borne perception. Psychology defines perception as a single unified awareness derived from sensory processes while a stimulus is present. That being said, consider a scenario where two people are exposed to the same experience at the same time. What if one of the two individuals had a past violent experience and every time they saw a color or smelled a scent they were taken back to the traumatic event on a subconscious level? Would their trauma subliminally impact how they witness an event when that color or smell is involved? Could two witnesses to a single event have very different depictions due to subconscious influences from past experiences?

As a little girl, I was one of two people witnessing the same event who walked away with a very different accounting. Most of my life I held that difference to be a lie, perpetrated by the other witness as they told their version of an experience. "I was there, that's not what happened" was my internal mantra but I refrained from speaking up since the other witness was a relation of mine. I was taught to be honest but also to be respectful, and if the inaccurate description did no harm, I believed it better to keep my mouth shut, a youthful indiscretion on my part. Lying is a slippery slope, once we get past the initial guilt of misleading another because it doesn't seem that important, eventually has the opportunity to provide an excuse for far more consequential behaviors.

The Lie

The lie most always remembered as truth falls dead in its track
A deadly sin, as a man begins, his fall from grace in this human race
Learned behavior or innate defect, to tell the lie, truth to reject
No difference found now, for to lie no longer breeds
No loss of self-respect, only fuel for inner greed
Mores lost, truth rarely found, in this Communication Age
Society spinning out of control, on life's ever-changing stage
Spirits fallen victim, lay littering our streets
As people pass, more lies are told, to all they meet and greet
This false pretense, a ruse for you lose, placing self above
Are these words reminding you, of your own narcissistic love?
No light or airy thought to see, in these words you now do read
Can you not see, to lie is cruel, disregarding life's most golden rule?
This bluish hue envelopes me, an attempt for my

mind's eye to see
Search then try to reason why, we tell the lie, truth
to defy
I myself make the effort to avoid, guilt rises in me,
as truth is destroyed
Yet occasionally fear does make its call, and into
the lie, I too do fall.

07.23.01

Moving around the country and working in a variety of sub-cultures offered up questions to my held beliefs of this truth vs. lie aspect of human behavior. What if their accounting was not a lie but rather the truth as they saw it? What if when this occurs, we acknowledge the difference and then explore why they see it so differently? Instead of building a barrier that divides truth from deception, what if we build a bridge that allows for a conversation?

This intent is not to decide upon who is right or wrong, but to allow the creation of an understanding that encompasses perception. Take away right, remove wrong, and what would that leave us? We have all been domesticated to these opposing forces regardless of the culture of our birth. The opportunity to discuss difference is the opportunity to evolve our experience, discovering self-truths while allowing for possibilities of different paths to the same destination. In other words, one can follow Buddhism, another Christianity, and a third Hinduism with all returning to the same source, the Divine's SoZoki, which awaits you in the coming pages.

Questioning Conventional Wisdom

We all have a story, a string of events and experiences that comprise our existence on this blue planet we call Earth. The spirit and body, a medley of energy mixing together in a perpetual dance until we take our last breath, and then slide into what? A question for the ages, each with our own ideas & beliefs often filled with unfavorable opinions formed without knowledge, thought, or reason, we just feel them to be right.

Seeking facts on life after death of the body is a slippery slope when one claims to know what occurs. We are familiar with the favored belief in Christianity; fanciful stairways ascend to a place where everyone beloved in a life reunites in their Earthly form, often referred to as heaven. Yet other belief systems do exist and not all are based on traditional religious tenets, but rather on philosophies where punishment for sins committed in life don't follow after the spirit leaves its corporeal shell.

I came into this world on October 10, 1956. There is no time on my birth certificate; the Navy didn't seem to think that the time mattered, so I have always relied on my father's estimate. It makes it challenging to really know how the stars were aligned at the moment in time of my birth. The closest estimate I have is early morning, after midnight and before dawn. My mom always thought it was after the sunrise, but my dad said there were no windows, so she really had no idea. I entered this life bringing confusion with me, and thus I have struggled to make sense of this world since my arrival.

I was raised in a family that practiced Catholicism. My father's practice was nothing less than staunch, a firm believer in the church to the point of being ordained an extraordinary minister. In southeast Alabama, the parish was considered a missionary as the membership was minuscule compared to the Protestant representation. Our priest visited many of the surrounding towns to provide the Mass to the small congregations and when he was absent from our church, my father would lead the Mass and provide communion, thus fulfilling his ordination.

My father also contributed his talents by installing the plumbing and electrical systems when the congregation grew, and a larger building was constructed to meet the needs of the expanding religious community. He taught religious classes referred to as catechism, and I found myself in his class while in junior high school. Unfortunately for my father, I was his Doubting Thomas, always questioning the instructions set forth by the Catholic church. It was only when I was in my early 50s that my brother shared a perspective of my early views on life.

My brother Victor was nine years older – I say *was* as he has passed – and had left home after graduating high school at 18 years old, returning only once to live with our family in his early adulthood. I give this bit of information to point to the fact that I was nine years old when he moved away. So, when he shared with me the following, I can reasonably conclude I was a young child. He told me that the thing he admired most about me was "your early questioning of conventional wisdom." I had thought my questioning occurred during adolescence, a time in life when resisting authority is a developmental process to gain autonomy, but with my brother's insight, I discovered my questions began atypically early.

I am certainly not proposing my questions were Divinely guided. I shared because I appear to have arrived with many questions for the life teachers that surrounded me. Could my early view of the world have produced questions, not to answer my own curiosity, but to influence the reflections of my teachers? To examine their unabashed acceptance of beliefs that had been passed on to them?

Influence of Events

Understanding, or at least having some insight into the influences and experiences of my entry into adulthood, is the best way I can show how I came to the beliefs and world views I hold today. As I share these experiences, it is important to note that most of what is presented here occurred prior to the invention of the Internet. We did not have cell phones, and our cameras required film that had to be developed with the exception of Polaroid instant gratification. We typed on typewriters, wrote letters, and made occasional phone calls to loved ones who lived afar, but paying long distant rates limited communication. Military families went months without hearing from their loved ones, and when they did receive letters they were frequently heavily censored. Our perceptions were mainly formed by experiences we personally witnessed, unlike today when social media intervenes and sways opinion, often steeped in inaccurate or fabricated storyline details. I am a member of a generation that was accustomed to delayed gratification. It taught most of us patience, a virtue earned not bestowed, and severely missing in many today.

One of my favorite musicians in my late teens and early 20s was Jimmy Buffett. Being a native of Pensacola, Florida, the daughter of a sailing naval aviator, and growing up on or near the beaches of the Panhandle, it was natural for my free-spirited approach to life to lend an ear to the storytelling he performed through his songs. For those who are not aware, he has been writing and performing his *island escapism* lifestyle of music since the early 1970s. As I graduated from high school, he was releasing his album *Living and Dying in ¾ Time*.

He followed up a couple of years later with his album *Changes in Latitudes, Changes in Attitudes*, and I continued to hear in his stories something that held true to my growing worldview perceptions. And as I traveled as a nurse in the 1980s, it became my theme song. Our society in the United States of America, our experiment in democracy, had become a melting pot of human cultures and religions from around the globe, and we became the ultimate representation of diversity. Each person, every family, wove their history of both domestication and genetic inheritances, creating the fabric of our forefather's ideals.

Completing nursing school in 1982 I began to acquire work experience. I give detail of the events that shaped my career in the chapter addressing synchronicity but will touch on a few items here as I share this section on perception. My first job as a registered nurse was in a neonatal intensive care unit, and the following year I was trained as a specialized nurse in the operating room. After a couple of years, I was ready to spread my wings, as any good military dependent is trained to do, with the ever-occurring triennial relocation known to us as "the three-year itch."

My first surgery department was in a community hospital that offered many but not all surgical services available, so I headed to New Orleans and Tulane University Hospital. This opportunity only came about as one of my older sisters (Judy) was there as a traveling nurse, working at Charity Hospital in the Labor and Delivery department. While at Tulane I added the specialties of organ transplantation and cardiovascular surgery to my repertoire. I also was exposed to the blend of spiritual belief systems practiced by the multi-cultural inhabitants of the city of New Orleans.

Until this point in my experience, the familiarity I possessed was limited to the denominations that comprised Christianity, Eastern Orthodoxy, and Judaism. I gained an awareness of Vodun (Voodoo) practices streamed from the enslaved Africans seeking to retain the spiritual belief systems of their homes from which they had been torn, and that gave me perspective into their experience. If you have not read the book *Middle Passage* by Charles Johnson, I highly recommend it but heed this warning. If you have a sensitive psyche be prepared to experience some strong emotions as he puts you in the shoes of those traded into slavery and the suffering they endured.

After a year and a half, I had gained the work and

life experiences needed and was ready again to take my next flight in life as a travel nurse. Looking back, I am considered a pioneer in this application of practice in nursing. Because of population movement and limited specialty nurses, temporary work contracts that provided housing and higher pay, allowed nurses to see the country without having to sign up with Uncle Sam. I took my first contract at a hospital in the San Fernando Valley with housing in Los Angeles near Burbank & Universal Studios. My big take-away from the two-plus years I spent in the LA area was learning that it was not a place where I wanted to remain. However, it was while living in the LA area that I was exposed to indigenous spirituality. Despite the herculean effort of the federal government to limit or extinguish the Great Spirit and Shamanic practices – or maybe because of that effort – the beauty of their ritual practices captured my imagination.

As it became clear to me that life in the fast lane was not my preference, I took a contract in Honolulu, Hawaii, and there I experienced my first culture shock. Everything was on *island time* which translates to no one is in a hurry to do anything. I loved it! Though I arrived as a Haole (How-lee), that is, a Caucasian, because I was working as a nurse I was also a Kama'aina or resident of the island. That gave me monetary discounts and inroads to local opportunities denied to tourists. It was during my time spent hiking trails and snorkeling reefs of the islands of O'ahu and Maui that I incorporated into my understanding of spirit the integral role nature plays. While there were many tourists flooding the island in fast pursuit of their bucket list dreams, the local inhabitants were some of the most generous people I've yet to know.

3 - *Intuition & Synchronicity*

Changing Intention

My job as an interim nurse leader at a New Jersey hospital had ended abruptly, creating an unexpected opportunity to return to my home in Charlottesville, Virginia. I had been working away from my adopted hometown for almost five years, fortunate to go home on weekends. While I was unsure of the financial impact the lack of employment would have, I knew it was my spirit's desire for me to find a way to stay home. Still a bit overwhelmed with the abrupt change in my life, and not ready to start filling out applications with the local hospitals, I was also questioning whether it was time to change my specialty, or even continue with nursing at all.

Don't get me wrong. It wasn't nursing that I needed to rethink, it was hospital leadership culture. The higher I climbed up the career ladder the more I questioned the practices of some of those in senior leadership positions, an unwelcome insight into decision-making at the highest levels.

Browsing the Internet on my very first day home I found a local website that had been created in my absence from Charlottesville. A program called "Meetup" had been organized to give members of the community with shared interests the opportunity to connect with like minds and forge new friendships. Two scheduled gatherings resonated with my creative muses: *Energy Healing* and *Art*. So, guided by my inner voice I signed up for an *Intuition & Mediumship Circle*. I recognized the nudge I was getting. In the face of the abrupt ending of my most recent hospital appointment, I was determined to keep focused on any and all opportunities offered by the unexpected. It was Friday afternoon. I signed up and attended the next meeting on the following Monday night.

It was at this event that I met Paul McKinley, author of *Rules of the Spirit* and *The Energy of Forgiveness*, and his wife Ann. During the meeting, I talked about my professional experience – 36 years in surgical services at 21 hospitals – and how I had grown from clinical practice into leadership. My focus had been on one of the greatest challenges that hospitals face, patient flow (or the disruptions thereto), and the impact it has on both the surgical patient and the surgical team. Based on that information combined with my advanced nursing degrees – Registered Nurse and M.S. in Nursing –

Paul said he thought that I had significant insights to share. He encouraged me to write about the processes, procedures, and techniques I had developed as a surgical services leader. And noting that I no longer worked as a clinical nurse but rather as a consultant, he suggested I write a book and form a business to support dissemination of my ideas.

Life, it seemed, was providing me with the time to focus on such a great endeavor, and I embraced the idea. It started out fine. I captured the intended content by first outlining the chapters for the book. It would begin with a review of the history of the scientific method. I noted the centuries of work built on the brilliant discoveries of Galileo in the 17th century, to the LEAN manufacturing approach developed by Toyota engineers in the 1990s to identify and eliminate waste, and how that was eventually applied to the health care industry in the late 1900s.

I felt I was off to a good start, but my inner voice kept repeating that this was not the book I was to write. With this realization, the creative flow stopped. The prospect of finding 30,000 words or so to create a book-length explanation of my thoughts and ideas about surgical services workflow was discouraging. As an MSN I was familiar with the length of citations in scholarly articles, and I knew I could easily generate ten pages of references to fill out the manuscript, or... I could listen to my intuition. What was the book I was to write?

Retrospective Synchronicity

As I reflected on the book project, I began to recognize events in my life as examples of synchronicity, guiding me through the significant realms of education, marriage, and motherhood, and especially my nursing career.

For example, years ago nursing school students were required to pass the National League for Nursing Pre-Admission Examination (NLN-PAX) for would-be nursing students wanting to get into nursing schools. The school I applied to was very popular, requiring not only the exam but also an interview with an elected board who served to assist the school in choosing candidates with the highest chance of completing their studies and passing the RN board exams. I was told, however, that test results had been delayed, that a new company had been given the grading contract, slowing down the process. In 1980, grading handwritten tests took time. It would be several academic quarters before I could matriculate.

Two weeks before the fall quarter was to start, I received a phone call from the program director. My test results had been unexpectedly delivered to the school, I had scored very high and a space had opened up. If I could quickly take care of routine physical and dental exams, they would allow me to forego the board interview and start immediately, and that's what I did.

The final quarter of the nursing program required completing a preceptorship at one of two local hospitals, which would then hire us into the position for which we had trained. I applied for two specialties, operating room (OR) as my first choice, and neonatal intensive care (NICU) second. I took an offer of a NICU placement as there was no opening in either operating room programs of the hospitals.

Ten months after graduation I received a phone call from the other hospital. The assistant operating room nursing supervisor was cleaning her desk when her boss asked her to contact human resources (HR) and request they secure a nurse trainee. At that moment, her hand landed on my application in the drawer she was cleaning. It had never been sent to HR after all but had lain hidden in her desk. She felt it was a sign and she gave me a call to see if I was still interested. I didn't see the *sign* at the time but wholeheartedly accepted the offer. And so began my long journey in OR nursing. Events unfolded with synchronicity, first school and then again with practice.

As I looked back in retrospect, I could see the events that had synchronistically unfolded, first with my entry into nursing school and again with my entry into my nursing specialty. The next synchronicity occurred six years later when I met Mark, who would become my husband and father of my only child, Tyler. I was working in Ohio on a travel nurse contract and knew only the few people I worked with in the small, two-suite OR. Late one afternoon a surgeon I had been working with offered me a ticket to a music concert he was unable to attend. It was for Rockin' Sydney and the River Rats, a band I'd enjoyed when I lived in New Orleans, and I gladly accepted the offer. It was at this out-of-the-blue concert that I met my husband.

This amazing connection occurred when I had only three weeks before my contract was due to end, and I was trying to get an assignment in Australia. At the ripe "old" age of 32, I was beginning to wonder if I would ever marry and have a child. I was also determined to continue exploring life as much as I could. So, had I not attended the concert that evening, I would not have my son. I believe Creation guided me to Ohio, and then to the concert that evening, to fulfill yet another of my life's missions, for I do believe our souls come to Earth with intention.

Another synchronicity involves the advancement of my education from an Associate's Degree in nursing (ADN) to a Bachelors (BSN) and then a Masters (MSN). Synchronicities can occur over long periods of time.

I had started writing on energy healing, specifically

how Reiki was taught and practiced, in 2009. At the time my education was limited to the Associates degree I had earned in my original nursing program. I hoped to write a continuing education course for nurses which would incorporate energy healing into the nursing process, but I needed someone with a higher degree to add their name to my writing. I asked a fellow nurse with a Master's degree, who agreed to my proposal, and then I immediately experienced complete writer's block. Little did I know that less than six months later I would be looking over the shoulder of another charge nurse as he checked out a program to advance his own degree. He never acted on his inquiry, but I found myself enrolled in the program one month later. During the following two and a half years I earned both the BSN and MSN degrees, developing research and writing skills that would serve me in many ways. Looking over the shoulder of the colleague who didn't follow up led me to where I needed to go.

I passed the oral defense of my written research project on 12/12/12, earning the MSN, and in the fall of 2018, almost six years later, I found myself back to where the writer's block had ended my first attempt and the birth of this writing about energy healing began.

Contrary Thought

We all have doubts, even when we have clearly been guided down particular paths on our journey. A co-worker once asked me if I felt I was God-guided. I answered, "I don't feel God-guided. I believe I am God-driven because I can be very resistant!" Because sometimes it isn't only doubt that we experience, but rather objection to the path we are being driven down. Surely we have the gift of choice most of our lives; that is one of the aspects of humanity we all embrace: free will. However, it is that free will that allows making poor choices, even when Creation clearly has another plan for our life.

For me, one of those choices is that I would have preferred to be financially independent and a successful artist rather than a nurse. I draw fine pencil portraits from photographs and make every attempt to fool the eye, or as the French say, *trompe l'oeil*. When people first look at a portrait I have completed they think it's a photograph, and when I explain it is a drawing they ask why I am a nurse and not working as an artist. My answer has pretty much always been, "There are plenty of artists and not enough nurses."

"To See Her Smile" (2009)

Drawing by Nancy Anna Blitz

So I would recommend you go with the flow instead of resisting the synchronicities in your life. We are limited to what we think we know, while God has the big picture. We may not always like or enjoy each stage of our journey, but in the end, I believe we will be grateful if we allowed ourselves to be guided.

Sharing Our Found Truth

"It is better to choose what you say than say what you choose." This anonymous quote was sent to me by a friend. It seemed remarkably apropos to this situation.

For many, sharing experiences that differ from their domesticated belief systems is accompanied by fear of loss of respect and even of acceptance within their families or communities. A person living within a small and conservative environment that inhibits exploration of different religious beliefs or governing methodologies takes this risk and may learn to disregard intuition as a result. Passivity or idle thought, and behaviors that reinforce the limitations of the prevailing worldview, can manifest an experience that limits conceptual ability to consider difference.

I typically honor synchronicities when I recognize they are occurring. I am not always correct about the insights; sometimes failing to accurately predict what I believe to be the likely outcome. However, failure has not stopped me from discerning events that seem to fall into a pattern meant to send me in a certain direction on my life journey. If I don't share these insights, I risk missing an opportunity to discover meanings through the input from others that could benefit myself or those I love. Do I find myself disappointed when my predictions prove wrong? Of course! but not enough to ignore insights that events have given rise to.

A recent example surrounds the earlier mentioned abrupt ending of employment. Shortly after arriving home, while searching the Internet for openings for nurse leaders I came across a new listing. A manager position at the local community hospital had been posted just 23 hours earlier. Such positions rarely open, and I felt my job must have abruptly ended so that I would return home to manage this operating room. But after two weeks and two rounds of interviews, although I was told the team really liked me, the hiring director told me that the hospital had decided to fill the position from within the organization.

I was disappointed. Apparently I was wrong to interpret that the one job ending, and another opening were synchronicities impacting my life. Sometimes events just happen without apparent rhyme or reason!

But I do believe the attempt to find meaning is valuable. It gives us additional insight into our own lives. It's like using the *I Ching* or *Tarot* or the *Runes*. They don't have to be right or even "make sense" but they can help you to think in new directions.

What about the skeptics in our world? Does it really matter what they think in the long run? If you are reading this book then I was right in my intuition to write it.

Synchronistic events paved the path that led me here, writing what you now read.

My advice is to be open to new people, new directions, new ideas. That openness is a welcome mat to synchronicity, and the more you experience it and acknowledge it when it occurs, the more often it will happen in your life. It's an affirmation that you are on the right track, even if you don't know where it is headed.

Still skeptical? What do you have to lose by opening your mind? For that matter, is your life already flawless so you have nothing to gain? What might you do to make things better for yourself? Each event in life is subject to something gained or lost. Listen to your inner voice. That moment that comes your way is presenting an opportunity. Lighten up and allow yourself to be guided. Hold this thought in the forefront of your mind and in your heart. We often have to give something up that is dear to us before we achieve understanding. Most of us are not clairvoyant. We dream and desire but do not see the future despite making sure-footed steps. The French say, "C'est la vie." Such is life. And Horace, the Roman poet, said, "Carpe diem." Seize the day, meaning make the most of life. These expressions from far away and long ago are meant to help us onward in our journey, regardless of where we call home.

Right Time Right Place – Leslie's Story

So, I mentioned that I do not personally experience guides, angels, or deceased loved ones, but I do have a wonderful story to share. A young friend who passed too early in life found a way to get a message to me after her passing. I call this "Leslie's Story" and have shared it with many others since it occurred 20 years ago. It has never failed to inspire those with whom I have shared it, and I hope that you, too, find inspiration, peace, and a better understanding of our Holy Spirit.

While married and living in Ohio, I had the privilege to meet a wonderful young woman who had been diagnosed with metastatic breast cancer in her early twenties. It was an aggressive disease that she fought with all her might. As she received treatment and it went into remission, she was determined to make sure other young women knew that breast cancer did not limit itself to older women but attacked youth as well. She joined two surgeons who had begun giving free seminars around the state to bring breast cancer awareness to women of all ages. Leslie's presence, to attest to her early experience, gave voice to the reality for women in their twenties.

After a few years in remission and finally settling back into somewhat of a normal life with her husband, she got the terrible news of the return of cancer. It hit the couple hard. They had a vacation to a Caribbean island planned. Her doctors suggested they make the trip and upon return make plans for the next steps in her battle for life.

At around the same time a book had found its way into my world, *The Celestine Prophecy* by James Redfield. I'm not an avid reader, and the book was not the easiest, but I did manage to read the book in its entirety. Mr. Redfield had written a second book, a sequel to the first titled *The Tenth Insight*, which I found a much easier read. I set the spiritual adventure aside, though, to study hardcore science, because at the time I was busy with a requirement for my job to become certified in Advanced Cardiac Life Support (ACLS).

When I heard about the recurrence of Leslie's cancer, I thought she might enjoy and possibly benefit from reading the books. I stopped by her home and gave them to her, explaining that I found them a wonderful way at looking at the life of the spirit. She was seeking comfort from many directions and took the books with her to the island. A couple of months later she lost her fight with cancer and we never had the opportunity to talk about the books.

A little more than a year after Leslie passed, I divorced and moved from Ohio to Virginia to take a job as a travel nurse working for a Richmond hospital. It was a stressful time, away from my son, who remained in Ohio. His father and I, along with input from my child, decided it would be best for him to remain in the family home, the school, and hometown where he had made friends from birth. He had something I had not had growing up as a child in a military family, and as much as it hurt me, I wanted him to have that comfort and support. A hometown, with friends he had known all his young life and a strong sense of community.

With such big changes in my life, I decided to seek out massage therapy. Every other week I found some relief from my despair, if only for an hour. Each time I went I felt a bit guilty, as the therapist had to put a significant amount of her energy into getting the tension out of my body.

Along with my nursing job, I was working on my Reiki Master education, and each time at the end of the massage, I would channel energy to Pat, the therapist, attempting to make her feel better after the hard work she had performed on me. She was not privy to any details about my previous married life in Ohio, but she did know I was a mother missing her son.

I think it was the third time I saw her that Pat asked me about Leslie. Just before getting started, she asked me who Leslie was. I lay there face down on her massage table for a moment, and then shared with her that the only Leslie that came to mind was my young friend who had died the year before.

"Leslie is here," she said, "and she wants you to know something." Pat then relayed the message that Leslie had never had the chance to thank me for the books I had given her, and wanted me to know that they had really helped her at the end of her life.

This blew me away. Pat knew nothing about Leslie, about her passing the year before, or the books I had shared with her. And I had made a pact with myself a long time ago that if I ever experienced visual or auditory hallucinations, I would check myself in for psychiatric evaluation, rather than believe a message was being delivered from life beyond the limits of this world. I firmly believe that if Leslie had tried to get a message to me more directly, I would have presented myself to a psychiatrist rather than a massage therapist.

This story came full circle the following year, when I had the opportunity to share Leslie's story during a conversation with James Redfield in Virginia Beach. He expressed gratitude that I had shared his book with her, and her story with him, and he requested that I write it and send it to him, which I did.

4 - Intentional Thought

Positive Prayer

It was the end of June into July of 2018, when one evening the Intuition and Mediumship circle I had joined spent time focused on the health and safe return of the boys and their coach trapped in the Tham Luang cave in Thailand. Their plight had captured the world's attention. We were part of the powerful international outpouring of people from all nations, races and belief systems sending prayer and positive thoughts to the boys, their coach and the rescuers. One of our members had a beautiful smile on her face as she shared her intuition that all would make it out alive. We focused on the rain, with intention to slow the arrival of the impending monsoon downpour which threatened to further inundate the cave and drown those inside. I wouldn't suggest that the thoughts and prayers from our group and around the world were responsible – there was tremendous courage and purpose demonstrated by the rescuers – but the result was that everyone was safely removed from the cave.

Closer to home I can offer thoughts by surgeons and internal medicine physicians who have re-searched – and observed firsthand – the impact of prayer on the outcomes of health. As an operating room nurse, I know there have been many times when the surgical team observed that the patient in poor condition did very well with the procedure. The opposite also occurs, when patients in great overall health had unexpectedly poor surgical out-comes, for no medical reason the team could point to. Did those with unexpectedly good outcomes do so because they received support in the form of prayer? Did those with unanticipated poor out-comes not experience the power of positive thought?

Dr. Allen Hamilton, a Harvard-educated neurosur-geon, medical advisor to *Grey's Anatomy* and long-time skeptic of medical miracles and the power of prayer, changed his mind on this subject after 30 years of practice. Witnessing modern medical mira-cles prompted him to question his previous skepti-cism. He went on to write *The Scalpel and the Soul: Encounters with Surgery, the Supernatural and the Healing Power of Hope.*[1] Like myself and so many

---

[1] Hamilton, Allan J., *The Scalpel and the Soul: Encounters with Surgery, the Supernatural, and the Healing Power of Hope*, New York: Jeremy P. Tarcher/Penguin, 2008 (ISBN 978-1-58542-615-7)

other members of surgical teams across the country, Dr. Hamilton would not deny what he had experienced not just once, but time and again in his neurosurgical practice.

Dr. Harold Koenig, an associate professor of psychiatry and medicine at Duke University, authored *Handbook of Religion and Health*,[2] in which he analyzed over 1,500 studies on the effects of prayer on the human body. His research revealed that those who pray on a regular basis are less likely to become sick. He discovered that when hospitalized, those who did not attend church had an average length of stay three times longer than those who attended regularly. Among heart patients, those who engaged in prayer were more likely to survive surgery than those who did not. He also found that those who prayed exhibited lower rates of occurrence of cardiovascular disease, cancer, and strokes. Depressed patients had fewer mood episodes, with less pronounced symptoms, when they either engaged in prayer themselves or were the object of the prayers of others.

---

[2] Koenig, Harold, *Handbook of Religion and Health*, New York, New York, Oxford University Press; 2012. ISBN 978-0-19-533595-8

Let me insert here that when I speak of prayer, it is by no means limited to religious prayer. Nor does going to a church give greater power than non-religious people experience from their own private place of deeper thoughts and feelings; for instance, from communing with a photograph or the ashes of a loved one, or with Nature while walking in the woods or by the ocean.

Herbert Benson, an MD at Harvard University, has studied the effects of prayer on medical conditions for decades. His experiments identified the primary factor in prayer as a relaxing influence that reduces stress and provides hope, both of which promote healing. His MRI studies of people in deep meditative states identified activity in the limbic system that affected the entire brain, strongly impacting the nervous system, blood pressure, heart rate, and metabolism. He also found that when body functions become evenly regulated an overall sense of well-being results.

The Curse of Negativity

Is the power of intentional thought limited to a desire to heal, or if not to heal then to do no harm? Westerners have begun to accept the power of prayer, but have we truly considered its opposite, the power of negative thought? Do curses work? When we are angry and wish someone would "get what they deserve," when we think "what goes around comes around," when we apply our ideas of "karmic return" to others, do our inner intentions hold the power to influence a medical outcome? Are negative thoughts as consequential as prayer or positive thought? And if so, should we not be mindful about what we send out to the universe? Is poor health the result of internalized and externalized negative thought patterns?

I admit this is not an easy task, to practice mindfulness about our own thoughts. Rather, it can be very difficult. Despite decades of working on it I still find myself falling into negative thought patterns. I struggle to master the ideal of maintaining positivity, as I understand that harm to one affects all. How can I wish for something adverse that might then harm the innocent? In the current climate of our American divide I am challenged every day.

So, should we avoid influences that encourage negative thinking? One would think so, but if we merely avoid those influences, are we still encouraging growth of spirit and consciousness? For me the answer is no if all we have done is to manage to avoid conflict within our own conscious mind but relinquish the opportunity to understand the darkness. An ideal is a concept of something in its perfection, a thing or person conceived of as embodying noble or high character. Ideals must be striven for, and that includes the process of engaging with the negative, the shadow side, of things, as well as the positive.

A central concept in achieving positive thought is to recognize the difference between an opinion about another's behavior and a judgment of the person. As you witness activity of which you disapprove, do you find yourself not liking the person, or their behavior? Are you identifying the person, rather than the action, as bad? How would you feel if you yourself said or acted in an objectionable way and then forever after were labeled meanspirited or worse?

These are questions to contemplate as we walk our path from base human impulses to higher spirit consciousness. Every day opportunity knocks: Do you react with damning thoughts to others' actions? Are your words an honest reflection of your beliefs, or do you entertain negativity in an attempt to align yourself with a group, rather than stand the risk of ridicule? Is your mainstay of communication gossip? Do you change the conversation, or walk away refusing to participate when the talk takes an ugly turn?

We are all works in progress, evolving beyond our imperfections and frailties. At best we can choose to be aware, modifying our thoughts or speech because we do not desire to do harm. At worst we may be aware of harm and purposefully choose to remain silent. And the last thought I will leave you with on this topic is that all of this also applies to how you think and speak to yourself. Our inner voice has the potential to be our greatest supporter or worst enemy.

In both venues, we might remember the saying, "Love the sinner, hate the sin."

Nice Versus Kind

I taught my son early in his life what I believed to be the difference between "nice" and "kind." I wanted him to understand "being nice" typically meant expecting something in return, and that it was unacceptable not to be appropriately "thanked." When gratitude was not forthcoming, as they thought it should be, judgment was passed with the resulting attitude being a resolve to "never do that for them again."

Not only does this undermine the good, it also turns a positive action into a negative experience. This approach also applies to favors. Have you heard the expression "you owe me one" when someone has done you a favor? Or maybe "I'll help you if you help me," tit-for-tat behavior that allows help only if some kind of "payment" is made. Children are sponges! I wanted my son to absorb the idea that helping others should not be contingent on "payback" be it kind words or deeds.

I taught him that an act of kindness, in fact, was the opposite of an act of niceness. Kindness does not seek anything in return but is given without thought of receiving. He is grown now, known to be a good-hearted, kind man, and I am a grateful mother.

Acts of Kindness

A common thread of thought does create
It could be love, or it could be hate
Knowing this, one would think it to be clear
Yet hate resides in the mind of man, creating so much fear
Still many are the gentle souls, dwelling in this space
Not everyone is caught up, in our frenzied human race
Some here play a creative part, reaching out through their fine art
But most are simple loving souls, and through them, love continues to grow
Balance in the universe, some seem blessed while others cursed
My reason for this rhyming chorus
Is to plant a seed, watch it grow before us

A vine of love woven through all, not just selects few

Born of simple gestures, acts of kindness, spread by all of you

Certainly love will get us there, in our battle to become aware

As we awaken to the collective soul, awareness is born of how we should grow

Ensuring the babes of all who exist, will someday too plant a sweet kiss

Upon generations because of this vine, love born from kindness to release the blind

Not turn away and make life tougher, stop our words that cause another to suffer

Grace wins the day when all seek to find, the love of the soul found in all humankind.

3.2001 & 9.27.18 (revised)

The Rice Experiment

Dr. Masaru Emoto acquired international exposure in the film *What the Bleep Do We Know?*[3] with his

---

[3]Dispenza, Joseph, *What the Bleep Do We Know*, directed by William Arntz, Betsy Chasse and Mark Vicente (April 23, 2004);Phoenix, AZ, USA: Samuel Goldwyn Films; film.

experiments on the cellular structure of water. I will admit I was not aware of Dr. Emoto's rice experiment and did not recall his studies of the impact on the molecular structure of water by human consciousness until my friend Danielle brought it up in a recent conversation. A YouTube search produced many opportunities to view the gambit of believers to skeptics who have been intrigued to repeat the rice experiment seeking to support or disprove the reasons for outcomes. Just as a skeptic purports talking to plants and seeing them thrive over those without interaction is because CO_2 is expelled as we speak and it naturally enhances plant growth, the believer while unsupported by strict scientific experimentation holds a belief that superior growth is because of their positive energy interaction with the plant.

Knowing the human body consists of 50-75% water, I would suggest you give the Rice Experiment a try to see what you think and how you feel when you experience the outcome of this experiment. Are your words, thoughts, or actions harming someone in your life? Is there someone you know who is negatively impacted by perceived friendships, co-workers, or a boss? The power of thought, word and action do exist. How do you choose to think, speak, and act? Performing this experiment gives you an opportunity to contemplate over a period of time, as it takes a couple of months to complete.

The first step is to gather the supplies you will need: 3 pint-sized (16 ounces) mason jars with lids, roll of 1-inch masking tape, 1-cup measuring device, metal spoon, pen or marker, 2 pans (1 with a tight-fitting lid), rice and water. The first step is to sterilize the jars, lids, spoon, and measuring device, killing bacteria that could contaminate the experiment. This can be accomplished by boiling in water for 10 minutes or placing on a roasting rack in the oven at 225 degrees for 20 minutes. If you do not have a metal device that prevents the items from touching the bottom of the pot of boiling water, I would recommend the oven method. If using the oven, turn the oven off after 20 minutes but leave the jars, lids, spoon and measuring device in the oven until ready for use.

While the items are being sterilized, following directions on the rice you choose to use, cook enough rice to provide 3 cups. Once the rice is cooked remove items from the oven ensuring they are not contaminated, don't lay individual items on a counter, remove the roasting pan. Using the sterilized items transfer rice putting one cup into each jar and immediately closing it with a lid. Place a piece of tape on each of the jars, one labeled love, one hate, and one ignored. This is done to ensure you do not mix up the jars and everyone involved in the experiment knows what, if anything, to communicate to the jars.

Multiple times a day speak to the rice in the jar as it is labeled. The jar marked ignored will not have any attention paid to it. Separate the jars so that each is receiving the intended communication. This is a fairly long experiment so make sure you are going to be able to interact each day for 60 days. You can choose the words you wish to say to the jars, just keep the communication to what is labeled.

As previously mentioned, you can view this experiment on YouTube by searching for "rice experiment" to see the results others have shared. According to Dr. Emoto[4], it is actually the water in the rice that is reacting to your communication. The results from others who have performed the experiment include the love jar having had very little visible condensation, and the rice looking a bit old but not having any visible mold. The hate jar had considerable water condensation visible and black mold had grown in the rice. Finally, the jar that was ignored had some condensation and on top of the rice was a layer of white mold that appeared to have created a shell-like appearance.

---

[4]https://thewellnessenterprise.com/emoto/

5 - Dream Actualization

Dreams and Daydreams

Once awake, I'm up and ready to face the day, and maybe for that reason I've never had great dream recall. But I am a great daydreamer and have always valued the process of bringing a dream to fruition.

As for daydreams, when I was a little girl my dream was to be a ballerina, and I held fast to that dream for many years. I began taking dance classes at four years of age. It might surprise those who know me now, but I was a very shy child. The one time I felt bold was on stage, dancing in front of cheering families and friends of the dance school, many of whom were strangers to me. Unfortunately, I was put *en pointe* too early; so I entered junior high school wearing orthopedic shoes. My dream was cut short and I was left disappointed and embarrassed.

Little did I know that the loss of my dream would physically impact me for decades. I unknowingly held the loss in the small of my back, suffering episodes that would leave me on the floor for a week at a time, my back in full spasm. The first time it happened I was 12 years old and continued four or five times a year, until my early 40s. It was not until a read a book by an orthopedic surgeon who suffered from chronic back pain of his own that I learned to identify what actually was causing my pain. His book focused on reaching back in memory to identify what was occurring in life when the pain first appeared.

It was when my ballerina dreams ended. My inner, injured child stored that disappointment in my lower back, but once I identified the loss and allowed myself to acknowledge and then appreciate the new directions and new dreams, which eventually led to nursing, that the painful episodes stopped and have never returned.

Messages and Desires

We humans have a great propensity for pushing through almost any roadblock to achieve our goals. At least those humans of character. I recall reading of the many times that John Denver was turned away by the music industry time and again before his talent was finally recognized and he was offered a recording contract. Imagine, if he had given up, we would never have heard "Take Me Home,

Country Roads" or "Rocky Mountain High." Only through persistent belief in himself, bolstered by family and friends, did he finally achieve the accolades his music warranted.

There are times in life when we must simply endure, nose to the grindstone, to achieve what we know we should do. There are also many times when we ignore the plethora of opportunities Creation offers to change our path, but when it is ignored, disaster strikes, forcing us to deal with what we resisted. How do we know when we are being heroically persistent, and when we are simply stubbornly headed down the wrong path? For the benefit of others who may need to rethink their path, I will share a disaster from my own life.

In 2000 I became extremely disenchanted with my life as an operating room nurse. Earlier in my nursing career I'd been fortunate to participate in a profession that was focused on patients' needs for successful procedures and recovery. But by 2000, that focus had changed at many hospitals. Along with the change from patient name to patient ID number, patient needs were no longer the central concern. Additionally, we were encouraged to focus on meeting surgical requirements with minimal supplies and maximum time efficiency. Then after witnessing a surgeon break away from a procedure three times to negotiate with her real estate broker, I was disgusted and ready to change my profession. I would leave nursing if this was where it was headed. I took a summer hiatus to consider my options.

But when the money ran out, I had to begin negotiations again with travel nurse companies, and that is when Creation stepped in and pulled me up short. I was enjoying an evening with friends, singing and dancing, having a great time. It was on one of my last days of freedom before beginning a contract in a new hospital, in a new state, the following week. The evening took a terrible turn. I will never know why I was physically assaulted but I was left with subluxation of all of the vertebrae in my neck, a herniated and bulging disc at two cervical spine levels, and pulled muscles from the base of my head down my neck and spanning out across both shoulders. I literally could not hold my own head up. After five months confined to a chair while I waited to see if the discs would return to their natural position, I finally was ready for physical therapy, and two months later I began picking up the pieces of my life, which did not include nursing. There were limits on my ability to perform necessary actions required of a nurse. But I was given a gift once the pain was tolerable, and that was the ability to draw, something I had never done before. I share the details of my recovery in the introduction to meditation in the final chapter of this book.

It was a couple of years before I was able to practice nursing again. Looking back I realized I had become willing to do things I completely disagreed with for the sake of money, so when I returned it was to a permanent position in a university hospital where the honest, caring concept of vocation had been preserved, and the conversations over the surgical bed were focused on teaching and patient care rather than acquisition of real estate and fantastical vacations. I held that job at the University of Virginia for 10 years and felt really great about the work in which I participated. If not for the assault I endured, it's impossible to know whether I would have found my way to a professional niche in which I could practice with pride.

Completing the Bucket List

I have never had a bucket list for my life. A list implies we should limit experience to what is on the list. If our attention is on checking items off that list, what might we miss? When narrowly focused on a single plan of action, do we dismiss the opportunity to be guided onto a better path? Acknowledging limitations in our capacity to be open to all that exists, in turn allows us to become more aware of experiences we could never have otherwise imagined as possibilities. I'm not here to say bucket lists are a wrong approach, to fill life with interest in places and events that intrigue or satisfy curiosity, but I ask you this: Does your bucket list address your spirit, your soul? As you developed your list was there a conscious effort to ensure you sought understanding or enlightenment in the vast variety of cultures and customs found around the world? Did you seek to discover the unknown, to bring unexpected phenomena into your consciousness? As opposed to collecting matchbooks from famous watering holes.

Not having a bucket list to check off has meant my life has been led by Creation, or what is sometimes called Providence. In other chapters of this book, I share the influences of places, and the people who inhabited them, opening my eyes and spirit to the broad landscape of human experience. Those people and places exposed me to a variety of cultural practices and religious beliefs which have served to open my mind, my heart and my soul. Creation has taken me on a journey that I am now sharing with you in the hope that you will see that we need not necessarily stick to a set plan or bucket list to flesh out our life story.

So, briefly: I was born in Pensacola, Florida, and when I was two years old my father was stationed at Guantanamo Bay, Cuba for three years. My family returned to Pensacola for the final years of my father's active duty status in the U.S. Navy. Once retired he moved our family to Enterprise, Alabama where he would teach weather and aerodynamics in the Army/Air Force Aviation helicopter training program at Fort Rucker. I started fourth grade there and went on to complete high school before I took flight on my own personal journey.

Four days after I graduated high school I moved to Milwaukee, Wisconsin for a couple of summer months, living with my brother Victor's family and experiencing a large city for the first time. From there I returned to Enterprise and attended junior college. After two quarters I returned to Wisconsin for the winter semester and then went south to warmer weather. I landed in Chattanooga, Tennessee, where I lived with my sister, Judy, for six months before moving on to Birmingham, Alabama, where I got my first apartment at the ripe young age of 18, with help from my sister, Jane.

But I wanted to re-experience my place of birth, so I moved to Pensacola. I secured a bartending job, found an apartment, and spent my free time on the pristine beaches, working a second job in a t-shirt shop. In Pensacola I discovered my first organic food store and became aware of the importance of living a healthful life.

I continued my traveling lifestyle in Gainesville, Florida where I tended bar in a bowling alley, perfecting my *roll* with free games, and learning to play the strategic game of backgammon with friends attending the university. From there I moved to Cocoa and then to Merritt Island, Florida, teaching ballet to children and working in the radiology billing office for my brother-in-law. It was while I lived on Merritt Island that my mother convinced me to follow her lead into nursing. So I returned to Enterprise, to live with my parents and attend nursing school. As I shared in the preceding chapter, I got the job I really wanted in nursing at Flower's Hospital in the operating room after entering into nursing as a NICU nurse. After a couple of years, I moved to New Orleans where I worked at Tulane University Hospital for about a year and a half.

Once I had gained adequate academic experience, I began travel nursing. I worked in and around Los Angeles, moved down to Redondo Beach, and then journeyed to Honolulu on travel contracts.

Leaving Hawaii, I headed back to southern Florida, first Fort Lauderdale and North Miami Beach before moving up to Fort Pierce. After a couple of years, I decided I would take a contract in Ohio, not having spent much time in the northern states, and I accepted a contract in Marietta, where I met my husband-to-be, Mark. I undertook two travel contracts after that at Ruby Memorial, the West Virginia University Hospital, one just before my marriage and the second a couple of years after the birth of my son.

After ten years in Marietta, I felt my spirit was dying. I loved my son with all my heart but could not make myself feel the same way for his father. Please know Mark is a wonderful man and outstanding 'eye doctor'. We just weren't the right fit. Our friendship was not enough to sustain a lifetime partnership. We cannot make ourselves love someone any more than we can make ourselves stop loving someone. Experiences, both physical and spiritual, gave me the push I needed to make the painful choice, but to be clear, I continue to feel I had a choice then. It was that I could either continue my journey of exploration or condemn my spirit to languish in Ohio. While it is easy to make wrong choices, it is extremely difficult to make right ones. If making right choices were easy, we would live in utopia.

I returned to travel nursing and landed in Richmond, Virginia.

<u>Our Place in Creation</u>

I like to leave a window open so that I can hear the birds. Sometimes there is an early bird, trying his best to woo a mate with a pleading song in the wee hours. I wake, thinking, "Give it up. I'm trying to sleep!" Then, a smile finds my heart as I lie listening to the beauty of the song, hoping he reaches her the way he has touched me. How could I wish for anything else? In all my travels, nature has been an influence on my thoughts, often presenting itself in the form of birds. I stop, I look, I listen, I feel their beauty and I thank them for their presence in my world. Often, after that interaction, I find a feather as I continue my day. I've never felt the presence of other-worldly spirit guides or angels, I don't feel the presence of loved ones who have passed, and I've never seen a ghost. But nature, especially in the form of birds, has often interjected influence and understanding. We can find this, whether we travel widely or stay close to home, whether we chase daydreams or simply let life unfold. We are part of all that exists, not above, below or separate. Although we may feel we are Creation's greatest achievement, owners of fire and caretakers of this world, are we really? Where do we exist in Creation? I have pondered these questions, and perhaps you do as well, on this journey of life of spirit on earth.

6 - Energy Is Energy

The Power of Union and Communion

While working as a travel nurse in the city of Virginia Beach, I had the opportunity to spend some time at Edgar Cayce's Association for Research and Enlightenment (A.R.E.)[5] Located on the third floor of the main building was a spacious, naturally lit meditation room. The windows opened onto a panorama of the sandy beach, the Atlantic Ocean, and beyond to a distant, hazy horizon. Intervening houses and hotels were hidden from view by an outdoor wall. At the back of the room, opposite the beach view, hung a tapestry depicting the Buddha and illustrating the major chakras. As I communed with the ocean, I began to experience an intense energy field surrounding – and entering – my being. I vibrated, then shook, sitting in my chair between the Buddha and the sea.

---

[5]https://www.edgarcayce.org/about-us/virginia-beach-hq/

Later that day, I had an appointment for a therapeutic massage at The Heritage Center. All of the resident therapists were required at that time to take the basic Reiki course offered at A.R.E. as a prerequisite to practice. Pat – another Pat, a male therapist – entered the room, and stopped to "set his intention." Intention is a prayerful pause to intentionally create the mind set with a desire to produce a positive outcome for the person from the session.

Aware of the Reiki training requirement and feeling the familiar energy I had only previously associated with Reiki practice, I assumed Reiki energy was what I was experiencing. When the session was over, I inquired about the Reiki intention he had used. His response was a wonderful surprise. Pat had spent three years studying on a reservation with a Native American shaman learning the rituals and prayers of healing practice. He said the intention he had set with me was not Reiki, but rather a prayer he had learned there.

It was at that moment that I understood: energy is Energy, all flowing from the same source and available to those who seek it, regardless of their spiritual path. All practices of faith, be they one of the major formal religions, ancient indigenous beliefs or other spiritual practices found around the world, lead the seeker to one Creation/Source. Those who don't hold stubbornly to a belief in their truth as the only truth, can embrace difference, and this is an exalted achievement of the soul!

This chapter considers some of the disciplines (or practices) found in the realm of global medical arts, many of which arise from religious traditions and spiritual practices. Each discipline addresses the impact of individual free will on healing and promoting health.

A human life journey contains influences and opportunities determined by history and culture of one's upbringing, as well as by the socio-geographical incidence of one's birth. Even so, when we are given the chance to view our own culture through the lens of others, we might challenge our understanding of our original stories and insights. When we embrace difference, we grow in understanding. A broader cultural outlook can be the basis for greater empathy, and deeper compassion, for those who are, on the surface, unlike us.

Western Medicine

During the colonial era in America the average life span was 25 years; today due in large part to the evolution of Western medicine it is just under 79 years. While advances in medical research and medical technique have been exceptional, risky but preventable behaviors such as poor diet choices, lack of physical activity, consumption of nicotine products and other toxic substances, and excessive intake of alcohol continue to degrade quality of life and life expectancy around the world. With the advancement of early diagnosis and rapid intervention capabilities, deaths attributed to heart disease, for example, have decreased over the past several decades, but the rate of decline has leveled off in recent years. Individual behavior is determined by individual choice to a great degree, rather than by the advice of medical community, and so heart disease remained the leading cause of death in the United States in 2018.[6]

Cancer is the second most common cause of death in the U.S. Again, due to advances in early diagnosis and intervention, treatment and management of disease, many cancers no longer are considered a sure death sentence but have been corralled into a chronic disease condition. Prior to covid-19, the third leading cause of death was car accidents, and studies have shown that use of tobacco products is directly related to all of the top three. Despite public education campaigns including dire warning labels on nicotine products and targeted legal attempts to prevent early consumption in teenagers, cigarette smoking and other tobacco uses often develop into addiction in adults.

---

[6]The top 10 leading causes of death in the U.S. - CBS News

Addictive behavior has many faces. We can also be addicted to love, or to allowing others to control our lives or sap our self-esteem. We all need to eat to live, yet food addictions contribute to a variety of diseases that impair or shorten our lives, including obesity, diabetes, hypertension, and heart disease. Workaholics, alcoholics, and drug addicts all employ denial of known risk, each behavior bringing with it a potentially devastating end result. The harm comes not only to the suffering addict but also to all those who know and love them. Behaviors often are duplicated in successive generations as children exposed to poor parental lifestyle choices replicate a cycle of destruction. Western medicine, with its allopathic or disease-focused and science-based practice, approaches its limits where matters of spirituality are concerned because it does not consider the whole patient as a holistic approach does, with the exceptions of doctors of osteopathic medicine and registered nurses.

Religion & Faith Healing

If we look back in time, we find many historical medical practices that have embraced spirituality as part of health and the healing process. In Chapter Four, I provided three examples of studies by prominent physicians of their experiences with the power of prayer on a patient's health. In combination with medicine, prayer is a powerful force for healing the body, moving past medical applications to counter physical issues and heal the spirit. The pain of the spirit can be just as intense as the pain of the body; neither should be dismissed as irrelevant. Those patients who benefit the most are those who are treated for both.

However, the consequences of pursuing healing through prayer to the exclusion of medical attention can be dire. An independent documentary film released in 2018 by Tom Dumican, *No Greater Law*, examines Christian faith healing based on the writings of the New Testament of the Bible. Faith healing is believed to be divine intervention in the life of an individual, elicited by prayer, ritual, and gesture for spiritual and physical renewal.

Shield laws have been passed in some jurisdictions to protect Pentecostal groups, such as The Followers of Christ in Idaho, from being prosecuted for child abuse when available modern, Western medicine is withheld from sick children. Denial of medical treatment is based on the belief that while death of the body may occur, the soul is with God. Some states, such as Oregon, have seen shield laws overturned. While most practicing Christians today embrace a combination of prayer and medicine, faith-based medical neglect does continue to occur, and children and adults alike suffer avoidable misery and premature death.

This unnecessary tragedy is not confined to the

United States, of course. It is far more prevalent in less advanced societies around the world where millions of people suffer and die due to medical neglect based on religious interpretation of healing practice. As with any aspect of faith, particularly religious faith, there is misinterpretation or misapplication. How many times did I hear my father say, "The road to hell is paved with good intentions"? We must be mindful about our intentions. Not only is history spotted with Hell's paving stones – e.g., the burning of witches in Salem – but even today, eleven of the United States do not have laws specifically prohibiting female genital mutilation (fgm).

Meditation

Today, the image of meditation as a transcendental hippie practice best performed while wearing loose, tie-dyed clothing is obsolete. Medically accepted as a complementary approach to medical health practices, meditation is now often recommended by Western medical practitioners as an adjunct to prescriptive medicine. Improvement in energy flow can occur during meditation, and both body and mind benefit from the practice.

Also known as purposeful reflection or contemplation, meditation is practiced world-wide with religious, spiritual, and secular approaches. Variations in technique offer different benefits, so exploring and experimenting may serve very useful purposes as you begin to explore meditative practice. Mindfulness, for example, is a technique for bringing focus to the present, allowing the mind to experience thoughts, feelings, and sensations in the moment without judgment.

Transcendental Meditation uses a *mantra*, a special word, which through silent repetition, over time, leads to a state beyond thought and feeling. The Body Scan technique brings attention to each part of the body while employing focused breathing and has been shown to reduce negative thoughts. To deepen positive thoughts you can try the Loving Kindness Meditation (LKM) which focuses on the self, but then extends to social circles and beyond. This technique can help you during conflicts, producing positive thoughts about self and others. Observing Thought-Mindfulness is another path to explore the nature of your ideations, positive and negative, and helps to stop ruminating, judgmental thoughts circling around in your mind.

Other approaches to meditation include

Kundalini, which focuses on tapping into your body's ethereal energy.

Zazen, which has you focus on natural but purposeful breathing patterns.

Mantra, the voiced repetition of a phrase, word, or sound.

With Gazing Meditation it is recommended you start with a short amount of time to prevent eye strain, beginning with 10 seconds of keeping your eyes focused on a natural object (not an electronic screen) and practice to extend that time to 10 minutes. Yes, without blinking, but you want to approach it slowly and carefully.

Guided Meditation works best for those with imaginative visualization capabilities, and it can be performed by yourself or with the help of a recorded or live presentation.

Mindfulness practices have been introduced to healthcare providers as a tool to improve inter-actions with patients and co-workers, in an effort to bring value to each interaction occur-ring within the stress-filled acute care hospital setting.

Meditation rooms have been established in many hospitals for both patients and health care providers alike in an effort to reduce and relieve stress.

Believing that meditation holds the promise of posi-tive outcomes, I still felt it important to research any negative impacts of the practice for this section. As I developed the topics brought forward in this book, I've attempted to provide only factual information and present it from a non-biased perspective. It doesn't take more than a Google search to find in-formation on the Internet, however, that does not mean all the information you find is sound. I would recommend you narrow your search to scholarly articles, created for research and academic learning and, importantly, subject to rigorous peer-review before publication.

There have been studies to investigate negative impacts the practice of mediation can produce as an unintended outcome. While the population at large benefits from meditation practice there are some reports of the practitioner experiencing anxiety. This can occur when someone begins their practice overburdened with concerns about correctness of methods, facing buried anxieties, or striving to experience white light, a space in the universe of positive energy. Such anxieties can be mitigated with help from a well-trained teacher who assists the student in developing an individual practice that reduces over-expectations – maybe by eliminating the concept of *perfect practice* – and very importantly, teaching self-compassion. The would-be mediators must understand that meditation is not – and does not replace – psychotherapy.

For those interested in finding more information on the benefits of meditation on a wide variety of diagnosed health disorders, the Science Direct website offers specifics provided by medical experts and researchers. This scholarly resource provides, for example, chapters from notable texts published by Integrative Medicine, Clinical Sports Medicine,

Developmental-Behavioral Pediatrics, Practical Management of Pain and Core Psychiatry.

While there are multiple approaches to meditation, it is important to set attainable goals as you begin whichever technique you choose. The purpose across techniques is to calm the mind. This may not be as easy as it sounds. What you think about your thoughts and what method you choose directly impact your practice. If you are looking for a quick fix you most likely will become frustrated as mediation is a practice that requires an investment of time and a commitment to focus. Understand that when you begin meditative practices, it may take a number of sessions to find one that works well for you; you may change practices, and ultimately it can take many sessions before you are able to calm your thoughts. Know this too, that if you stick with it, with the right teacher, your ability to go to a place of serenity in your mind will grow, and the benefits are lasting.

In the final chapter of this book, I share my own experience with meditation. I also provide a non-guided process that works well for those who find difficulty in calming their mind, or who have not had success with other methods. It incorporates both the Zazen and Gazing techniques, using intentional rolling breaths while removing all stimuli except the flame of a single candle. Also included in that chapter is the SoZoKi Guided Meditation to assist you in channeling Creation's energy, with the intention of feeding both the ethereal and the physical body. But I trust that I have here already provided enough information to incentivize you to begin the search for the technique that works best for you.

Indigenous Shamanism

What is a shaman, where do they live, and how do they heal? Shaman is a word originally from Siberia, meaning one who sees in the dark or one who sees hidden realities. Moving into an altered state of consciousness, shamanic healers access the realm of spirit to bring information and healing to the person seeking help. Shamanic belief holds that all problems, whether they manifest as physical, mental, or emotional, are due to spiritual imbalances, and restoration of balance in the spirit realm will translate to healing in the material realm.

It is believed by some that shamanism is the oldest practice of healing, dating back 30,000 years. Indigenous cultures in Northern and Central Asia, North and South America, Australia, New Zealand, Northern and Eastern Europe and Africa practice ancient spiritual healing arts. Shamanic practice may even predate the migration of humans across the globe. Despite differences of geography and culture, shamanic practices would feel surprisingly familiar to practitioners from all corners of the Earth.

I discovered this for myself as I was recovering from my neck injury. One day, on the way to a medical appointment I was inexplicably moved to explore a small, unfamiliar bookstore. After spending some time browsing, I was about to leave empty-handed when a book on shamanism caught my attention. Remembering my energy experience in Virginia Beach, I pulled the book off the shelf and purchased it. Later, waiting in the doctor's office, I began reading the forward. It described the first contact between a shaman who had survived in isolation behind the Iron Curtain with other shamans from around the world. As they interacted, they discovered common practices that crossed cultural or tribal differences. The shamans embraced the rich rituals shared by their counterparts, rather than dismiss because of differences.

The shaman archetype, no longer limited by indigenous genealogy, or geography, now represents a broad diversity of nationalities and lifestyles which share an approach to healing based on rectifying imbalance. Methods employed by such healers include spirit journey, soul retrieval, removal of undesirable energies, soul memory recall for past-life healing and ancestral lessons, soul-assist cross over, chakra illumination, aura cleansing, and hands-on healing. Shamans often make use of spirit guides or guardians, and animal or plant allies as they travel into the spirit world.

Ayurvedic Medicine

From the Vedic culture in India comes the 5,000-year-old system of Ayurveda. The name is derived from two Sanskrit words, *Ayur* meaning life and *Veda* meaning science or knowledge of all aspects of life, and Ayurvedic medicine is the primary medicine practice in India. It includes guidelines for ideal life routines, both daily and seasonal, as well as diet, proper attention to the senses, and the integration and balance between spirit, body, mind, and the environment.

Three fundamental energies – movement, structure, and transformation – govern the outer and inner environment, according to the Ayurvedic viewpoint. What we call mind and body are products of *Kapha* (Earth), *Pitta* (Fire) and *Vata* (Wind) which determine our body type. While all three *doshas* are present in each of us, typically one or two will dominate. When *Vata* is dominant, the body tends to be thin with a light, energetic, enthusiastic, and malleable mind. When *Pitta* is dominant, we are goal-oriented, intense, and intelligent with a strong desire to live life to its fullest. The *Kapha* body is likely to be heavy, slow, and steady.

Substances used with Ayurvedic medicine include herbs which are sometimes combined with minerals, metals, and other materials, and is called *rasa shastra*. When improperly or carelessly used, these do have the potential to be harmful and toxicity can occur. Many of the products employed in Ayurvedic practice have not been studied in clinical trials and are considered dietary supplements in the U.S. A study performed in 2008 funded by the National Center for Complementary and Integrative Health (NCCIH) examined 193 products common to this medical practice, and found 21% contained levels that exceeded acceptable standards for mercury, lead or arsenic. Just because you can find a product for sale on the Internet does not mean it is safe to use! Even if recommended by a qualified Ayurvedic Medicine practitioner, before using products which are new to you consult your local pharmacist to be sure they are safe to consume!

Studies on the effectiveness of Ayurvedic approach for the treatment of diabetes and schizophrenia have been inconclusive but encouraging. Researchers at NCCIH began clinical trials in 2011 comparing a total of 40 Ayurvedic herbal compounds with methotrexate, a conventional treatment for rheumatoid arthritis, and found both provide similar effectiveness. Turmeric is an herb often employed by Ayurvedic practitioners for inflammation, and studies, while limited, show that it may help arthritis as well as some digestive disorders. Another preliminary trial tested the resin *Boswellia* (frankincense) as a remedy for arthritis and showed it to have immune system-boosting and anti-inflammatory effects.

Acupuncture

As early as 6,000 BC, Chinese practitioners of medicine may have used sharpened stones and bones to perform the treatment of acupuncture. Other records reveal that primitive needles were used as early as 1,000 BC, and the earliest documented use was described in a publication, *Inner Classic of Medicine* or *Nei Jing* during the Han dynasty in 206 BC. Authorship is attributed to the Yellow Emperor Huang Di.

In acupuncture practice, needle placement is determined by the therapist's choice, in consultation with the patient, of lines of meridian or energy highways that access all body parts via many points along their paths. Meridians exist in corresponding symmetrical pairs on each side of the physical body, comprising 14 complementary pairs, one *yin* with an upward energy flow, and the other *yang* with a flow of energy downward. There are also two single mid-meridians, the anterior Conception Vessel or *Sea of Yin*, running up from the pubic area to the mouth, and the posterior Governing Vessel or *Sea of Yang*, originating in the tailbone and running up the spine, over the top of the head and ending at the mouth where it meets the Conception Vessel.

While the practice of acupuncture has been used as a healing treatment to balance energy flow, it has also been used as a surgical anesthetic in China. In the early 1800s, articles appeared in American medical journals describing acupuncture practice, but it was not until 1971 that understanding and acceptance began to occur in the U.S. Several events, including President Richard Nixon's historic trip to China, took place around this time. President Nixon was accompanied by his physician, Major General Walter R. Tkach, MD, who upon returning home submitted an article for the July 1972 issue of *Reader's Digest* titled *I Watched Acupuncture Work*, compelled by the effective uses of acupuncture he had witnessed. Also in 1971, James Reston, then vice-president of the *New York Times*, underwent an emergency appendectomy while reporting from China. Acupuncture was the anesthetic used and he remained awake for the entire procedure, which he wrote about on his return to the US. The third notable 1971 event occurred when New York surgeon Dr. Samuel Rosen had the opportunity during a visit to China to observe acupuncture anesthesia, later reporting that he could not explain medically how the application worked.

As a result of these reports investigating teams from the U.S. went to China to observe a variety of surgical procedures including kidney surgery, cesarean section, open heart surgery, dental extraction, and tonsillectomy. The patients remained not only awake but alert during the entire procedures, although no Western anesthetic agent was used. The placement of the acupuncture needles never interfered with the surgical sites and were placed without apparent Western anatomical relevance. Deep precision placement needles in Chinese acupuncture is far more invasive than our experience in the States

Subsequent research in the U.S. and around the world unraveled the acupuncture mystery, finding that the needles stimulated and caused the release of the neurotransmitters serotonin, y-aminobutyric acid, dopamine, and norepinephrine, as well as polypeptide analgesic enkephalins, which explained the pharmacologic and biomedical effects known to Western medicine. In 1997 the American National Institutes of Health declared there was sufficient evidence to expand the use of acupuncture into conventional medical practice.

Advantages of acupuncture, when compared to a general anesthetic, include the lack of needed expensive equipment and personnel to monitor a patient. There is no hangover effect – patients do not experience physiologic depression, nausea, or vomiting – and there is no potential interference with antihypertensive (high blood pressure) or other conventional drugs. There is no risk of developing an air embolism, it does not cause vascular spasms or cosmetic problems, and patients do not experience emerging delirium seen in the recovery from a general anesthetic. Disadvantages include patients who do not respond to acupuncture (15%), a longer induction time requirement, the opportunity for increased blood loss, absent amnesic effect and satisfactory relaxation, and the possibility that needles may interfere with the surgical site.

Indications for acupuncture use include allergies to local or general anesthetics, as well as serving as an adjunct to local or general anesthesia. Patients who object to dental injections, have an abscess causing local acidosis in tissue or an abnormal airway or other deformity stand to benefit from the use of acupuncture rather than a conventional anesthetic. The fear of loss of consciousness and the presence of common cold symptoms, sinus problems or respiratory disease that can inhibit use of a general anesthetic are also indications for acupuncture.

My personal experience with acupuncture coincided with me writing this book. As a child I had a fear of needles, in part due to being stuck frequently for required vaccinations as a military dependent. Acupuncture was the last thing I sought as a medical option...until I realized I needed to reduce the amount of hormone replacement I had been taking for years to combat hot flashes. Women experience frequency, intensity, and duration of menopausal symptoms on a bell curve, and many find that these symptoms recede in time. I am not one of them. I had always suspected that my "inner thermometer" was broken, and science finally unlocked the mechanism and proved my thinking correct. It turns out that, in women who experience severe flashing, the hypothalamus has essentially collapsed, allowing very small shifts in temperature to cause full-blown attacks that begin with a massive wave of nausea, followed by burning skin sensations and finally a sweat that drenches the entire body. Without hormone replacement therapy (HRT) it can occur many times throughout the day and frequently during sleep. I was taking a milligram of estradiol in the morning and then another at night to keep my body regulated, ensure adequate sleep, and keep myself presentable during the day.

A new gynecologist warned of an increased risk of stroke on HRT in my 60s, and recommended an off-label use of a low dose of Effexor, a strong central nervous system medication used to treat anxiety. I gave it a try but after one dose I experienced severe nausea and blurred vision that lasted for 72 hours. So, I decided to put my research skills to use and began looking for an alternative. I unearthed a study that compared Effexor to acupuncture and found acupuncture to be as effective as the drug, with results lasting after acupuncture stopped, while symptoms returned in the Effexor patients as soon as the medication cleared their body.

Fortunately, in my hometown an opportunity existed that provided a shared acupuncture experience that significantly reduced the cost of treatment. The first time I went, I met with therapist Sara Beth, who was a godsend. I explained the reason for my visit and shared the research on the hypothalamus that I had found. After one acupuncture session I was able to reduce the medication to a single milligram each day. A few weeks later I was able to reduce it to one milligram every other day. Since beginning the sessions I have not experienced the severe flashing that I had suffered for the previous six years of my life. Thank you, Common Grounds in Charlottesville, Virginia, for offering the opportunity, and Sara Beth for her generosity and amazing therapeutic ability!

7 - Reiki

My intention for this chapter is to share my own introduction to Reiki, a practice which, among other things, emphasizes the understanding that not all healers are saints. Healers experience many of the same circumstances as non-healers, not always making the best choices out of those that present themselves. None of us walks this journey free from mistakes. You, too, are certainly worthy and capable of accessing Creation's energy regardless of your past; awareness is the essential first step to understanding how the energy of the spirit heals in a body/mind continuum. Through sharing my experience, it is my hope you will be inspired to find your soul's path back to SoZoki.

I have purposely left out the real names of many people in this chapter. I share the impact their actions have had on me to demonstrate the connections between our physical and emotional health throughout our lives. Many of our aches, pains and overall diseases date back to earlier life experiences. We experience a physiological chemical release when threatened' this is known as the "fight or flight" response. We similarly respond to loss, disappointment, and emotional injury in our minds this way. Because our psyches can contain only so much pain or conflict, we move excessive emotion into our bodies, which then manifest as the physical symptoms of illness or injury. Too often we fail to bridge the connection between prior experiences and current health disorders.

What is Reiki?

Reiki is two Japanese words, *Rei* meaning universe or universal, and *Ki* meaning energy, and it is pronounced as Ray'-key. Reiki Ryoho is a practice developed by Mikao Usui (1865-1926), although his practice may have been one of many performed, as healing was a popular movement away from the consumption of medicines. Varying chronicles of his actual experiences and reasons for the birth of Reiki are the result of World War II's destruction of any potential validating documents. One common thread as for intent of the practice, Mikao Usui is thought to have been of the opinion that it should be free to all peoples to help them advance their spiritual awareness to heal their spirit and therefore their body. Regardless of the initiating events or validity of origin, the point is that we humans have for millennia recognized and have turned to energy to assist in our health and healing of mind/body/

spirit (aka: soul).

I have developed *Ésprit with SoZoKi* – it translates to *Lively Spirit with Creation Energy* – as an individual, independent practice that reacquaints you with an age-old approach to acquiring awareness and advancing you on your spiritual evolutionary path. As a student of this practice, you will find yourself able to lead your own energy work through the application of your knowledge base and techniques acquired. The chapters that follow will take you through the narrative of events that led to the development of *Ésprit with SoZoKi*.

Revelation & Exploration

Energy healing entered my life in the late winter of 1998 and early spring of 1999. A variety of threads in an overfull life wove a veil that clouds my memory of that difficult and pain-filled but nonetheless fertile time. I do know that I had cut back the time I spent working as a nurse but increased volunteer hours at my son's school. At the same time, I made some health decisions that would lead to completely unexpected course corrections in my life.

To begin with, because age was shifting teeth forward in my mouth, my dentist thought I would eventually have problems with my bite if I did not take quick action. I accepted his referral to an orthodontist. Upper and lower braces were applied to reorient my teeth, along with what is called a thermal wire to speed the process. Those who have worn braces know the sensations associated with this hardware, and many report dreams of their teeth being so loose they fall out on their own. In the process, I learned I had an allergy to nickel, the metal used to make the thermal wire.

At first, I was diligent about keeping dental wax covering the metal to prevent tissue irritation. I thought I was having a normal response to the new surfaces against the soft tissue in my mouth, but when I went to my next appointment the following month the orthodontist was alarmed by the reaction he saw. He questioned me about allergies, and I acknowledged that my mother and sister reacted to nickel, and that I couldn't wear costume earrings, only silver and gold. This confirmed that I needed to have the wire removed immediately.

He suggested wires that did contain nickel but which would work more slowly. However, in the first month with the thermal wires, my teeth had been pulled back to their original position although my mouth was so sore I could barely eat. I asked that he take everything out at that appointment. I would live with my teeth as they were and hope they would settle and remain in the correct position. I wore a dental retainer for several months, but pain continued to inhibit my appetite. I was losing weight and beginning to be concerned about my overall health, and eventually stopped using the retainer as well. It was months before my teeth felt secure in my jawbone. While my mouth was changing so was my vision. (Isn't aging great?) I was married to an optometrist – sigh – but as we all know the plumber's pipes are the last to be repaired. The care of the eye doctor's wife is hardly different. He was and is a great doctor, beloved by his patients. But instead of having to go into his office to have the new glasses fitted and checked, I found them conveniently brought home and placed on the kitchen island. I put them on and immediately struggled with the new no-line bifocal set in the small frames I had chosen. As nausea set in, he reminded me that it could take a week or so to get use to the new lenses. I gave it my best shot.

Now I had a sore mouth and nausea as well. I lost my appetite, shed a few more pounds, and felt myself to be in a constant state of imbalance. I can see all these facts from a distance, clearly identify what had caused the change in my state of health, but at the time I could not put the pieces of the puzzle together. Then, inexplicably, the palms of my hands began turning red and burning. The only relief I found was to put my hands under cold running water. There was no discernible pattern as to when they would turn red and burn, but as a nurse – as a human being! – I knew that it was not normal.

I saw a doctor in search of the cause. Blood work to

test my thyroid and other hormone levels came back normal. My blood sugar tested normal as well. A physical exam revealed no explanation for what was happening to my hands. I requested a CT scan of my brain to rule out a tumor or an aneurysm. That too was normal. I came away perplexed and still sick.

Seek and You Shall Find

Meanwhile, I finally took the new glasses into my husband's office to see his optometric technician. I was still living in a world of nausea, long past the trial timeline for adjustment to the new prescription. That is when I learned that the frame was too small to hold no-line bifocal lens. I switched to two pairs of glasses, one for near the other for distance, and immediately the nausea stopped.

My mouth was finally healing, my appetite came back, and I was on the road to recovery, but my hands were still often red and burning.

It was around this time I received a phone call from a friend and colleague. She was aware of my health issues including the burning hands, and wanted to share some unusual personal experiences that she had previously kept to herself. In our scientific surgical nursing world she would have been ridiculed by colleagues for what she was about to tell me. She requested that I not share it with anyone, and I kept that promise for 20 years. Because I recognize that now Western approaches to healthcare are merging with Eastern energy practices, I feel it is imperative to share her late 20th century experience.

I must say the skeptic in me was alert as I listened to her story. If it had not been coming from a fellow OR nurse I would have politely listened and thought she was nuts, but I kept an open mind as I listened. She began by describing an experience that had occurred several years earlier. A great lover of animals, she had a pet who had fallen ill and was near death. Her little boy was extremely upset, and she was feeling much the same. Following her intuition, she held the animal and her hands became very hot, while she continued to hold the animal successfully wishing it back to health.

The second experience involving her hands occurred during a surgical procedure. It involved a large amount of what looked to be dying intestines in the patient, so much so the surgeon expressed concern about what the patient's prognosis would be if all the affected bowel was removed. My friend, serving as first assistant, asked if he would pause and allow her to lay her hands on the affected area. He agreed, and after a few minutes the bowel began to turn pink as blood flow returned to the intestines. He looked at her questioningly. She asked him and the other witnesses to keep her confidence. This was a time when most alternative modalities of adjunct therapies were not only questioned but ridiculed by Western medical practitioners, and she was afraid of what might be said about her.

Then, after relaying these stories she went on to tell me the reason for her call. An ad had appeared in our local paper announcing the opening of an alternative medicine center, and the owners were advertising a "Healing Hands" Reiki seminar. Curious, I signed up for the event along with my friend, but the night before the seminar, her babysitter canceled and so did she. I decided to go by myself to see what I could learn that would help my burning hands. Others who had signed up had also canceled and so I had the two teachers to myself. They were a mother and daughter-in-law new to the area, both Reiki Masters, and it was their first time to teach the program. I was the perfect student for them. Me of many questions, along with a healthy dose of skepticism, I had them thinking and reaching to answer my questions. I added, in turn, a great deal of anatomy and physiology particulars to their knowledge that day, as neither had formal medical education.

The day started with smudging sage, for both the room and each of us. This was followed by an audio-guided meditation of a traditional type, visualizing our feet growing roots deep into the ground, to attach to Earth's energy. (Meditation is not something that came easy to me then, and my skepticism persisted.) After the meditation they taught me the history of Reiki, sharing Drs. Usui's and Hayashi's and Mrs. Takata's stories.

They taught me the principles of Reiki, and reviewed ethics and treatment with Reiki, including the aura, the lines of meridian, the chakra system, and yes, the hand positions using the minor chakras located in the center of the palm to channel healing energy. This should have been an aha! moment for me, (red burning palms = energy vortex) but my inner skeptic was alive and well; okay, not well but loud. After all, none of this was based on Western scientific reasoning. But I kept listening. I kept learning, asking questions about the ethereal and providing answers about the physical body.

We took a break for lunch and when I returned I found a massage table had been set up in the room. The daughter-in-law was the first person to lie face up on the table, taking the role of patient/client as the mother took over the teaching role. They explained that Reiki does not require actual touch but allows hands to hover over the body at about six inches, enabling those who preferred not to be touched to nonetheless receive the benefit of a Reiki energy session.

To begin a session, the hands should remain off the body because the first step is to perform *Byosen Reikan Ho*, a technique used to scan the energy field for areas of disease or disharmony. We started at the head, both hands palm down, and began moving slowly down the daughter's body, trying to sense areas of heat that would alert us to an imbalance. I didn't feel anything as I did this but continued in my attempt to keep my mind open. Next, the mother and daughter-in-law changed places.

We began the scanning process again, starting at the head, and as I moved down, I felt a hot spot over the right lower side of the mother's abdomen. When I shared this, she told me she had had an appendectomy. Still the skeptic, I continued and felt another hotspot over her left knee. She shared that she had recently undergone left knee arthroscopy. My skepticism was beginning to fade.

Then I was the person on the table. After they performed a scan, they both began to channel Reiki energy to me. Hands were placed through the positions and after about 30 minutes they stopped and asked me to get up. As I stood up, I experienced an incredible lightness of being. I felt as though I was walking a couple of inches off the ground, filled with energy, unlike the lethargy often felt after a massage. (That sensation, by the way, is due to lactic acid released from the muscles as they are massaged.)

To attune is to bring into harmony or agreement, and this was the final step in my initiation to connect to Reiki energy, what I refer to as SoZoKi. (Many readers will know that the Japanese word *ki* means energy.) While it is traditionally recommended that four attunements be performed, Master to Student, each separated by at least four hours, my experience differed. I was warned that I might feel sick after the attunement, in the form of a headache, a cold, nausea or diarrhea, as the body aligns with SoZoKi consciousness, but I did not experience any such physical release.

Chapter 9 of this book is focused on self-practice, and there I emphasize the significance of rituals, to sustain knowledge of practice, as well as in daily self-energy practice. I do not believe that repeated attunement rituals are required to access energy for one's self or another person, but I do feel that an awareness of understanding of attunement benefits the novice practitioner.

Birth of an Imperfect Healer

Healers serve as examples to show that engaging our spirit energy with God's creation energy, SoZoKi, need not require membership in an esoteric community or religious order. Yahweh, Great Spirit, Elohim, Elah, Ilah, Supreme Being, God, Divine Design, Creator – whatever name you choose – is connected to us through our own Holy Spirit. A healer's path is not anointed at birth or ordained at a particular age on life's path. Many healers are skeptical when healing energy begins to appear in their life, and this was certainly my experience. I cannot recall how many times I said to myself, "Okay, it seems to have worked, but I'll bet it won't happen again."

When I look back at my life's journey, I see myself as a kind person, but of course there have been events that were perhaps not representative of good character. One that can serve as an example of poor judgment nonetheless taught me an important life lesson in my youth. In high school, I had friends across the continuum and did not identify with any clique. I preferred to choose my friends rather than have them chosen for me, not by my parents, and certainly not by my classmates. My approach could have been because we moved every few years, having to start friendships again and again, but in all honesty, I think it was something innate in me.

During my junior year, I played the clarinet in the band during concert season and was a majorette during football season. When a powder-puff football challenge was presented, I was asked to be on the majorette's team. In the '70s it was the girl's version of a flag/tag football game which I believe most are familiar with today. I accepted the challenge, knowing full well the girls intended to battle it out on the field with a group they did not like. During the game, I was injured, experiencing a hairline fracture in my right forearm, which meant I could not practice twirling a baton prior to the football halftime show.

To say that my band director, a stickler for perfect performance, was a little angry with me is an understatement. My parents were disappointed in my choice too, as I was in myself. I felt terrible that I had participated in an intentionally mean-spirited event, and I believed my injury was the result of my poor judgment. Lesson learned! I made up my mind not to succumb to peer pressure, but to fill my life with acts of kindness rather than meanness, and to encourage others to follow suit in their own lives.

This story may seem in itself insignificant, but my point is that God does not expect us to be perfect. In our imperfection, we still are bestowed with gifts from Creation to help ourselves and others on this human journey of spirit evolution. Just as parents forgive the child they brought into this world, and just as we forgive ourselves our missteps, our Creator forgives.

Uncertainty & Mistrust

Is it just me or have you too suffered from distrust? I believe I entered this world with trust issues. I say this because of the stories my parents shared with me. I am the youngest of four children and my siblings are Judy six, Jane seven, and Victor nine years my senior. As an infant, I cried whenever a stranger entered my world, not just those trying to interact with me but those who merely walked into the room. I am told the only person outside of my immediate family that I did not react negatively to was my mother's sister, Billie, and to this day she remains my favorite, and the only one left of her generation.

They said that as an infant and young child I would sit on the floor for hours, rocking forward and back. In a chair, or in a car, the rocking continued, and my family nicknamed my rocking "bumping." This went on for years, and I recall my brother saying, "Nancy, if you don't stop you are going out on your first date bumping!" Eventually, around ten years of age, I gave it up, but to this day I can pass hours in a rocking chair, to and fro, not noticing the passage of time. My strong aversion to strangers, along with the persistent rocking, reminded my mother of something she had learned in a child psychology course in nursing school. She came to the conclusion that I was borderline autistic. She told me that the hardest time we, mother and child, experienced in my early years, was when I needed new shoes. Not only did a stranger have to get close enough to talk to us, he had to physically touch me, and I would scream the entire time as if I was being abused. My mother would avoid the process as long as she possibly could.

As an active duty military family, and my father a lieutenant commander aviation squadron leader, my parents were expected to attend many social activities. This presented a problem. A babysitter was arranged, and my vocal objections would begin as soon as the sitter entered our house. I was two and three years of age when these struggles took place, so I had long passed the stranger anxiety that many infants experience. Eventually, my parents figured out if I was asleep before the sitter's arrival there would be no distress, and so we managed. Even today, I am reserved in social situations where I do not know anyone. Other than that, I am completely an extrovert!

By the time I was four I had lost some of my stranger anxiety, and around this time my parents introduced me to ballet classes. I loved to dance across the stage and did so without fear, possibly because there was no direct interaction with the strangers in the audience. Most people would have had a hard time believing I started out with so much fear of those unfamiliar to me.

While my fear of strangers diminished as I grew, mistrust was still a prevailing experience for me. Certain behaviors by others continued to play a significant role in my distrust. I can't tell you the number of times I witnessed someone speaking on the telephone, sounding as though they were very interested in the caller, yet at the same time making face and hand gestures that belied their words. For years I avoided the phone because I could not be sure the person on the other end really wanted to be speaking with me. In-person conversations were easier as I could witness positive engagement for myself. I recall my mother pushing me as a teen to make my own telephone calls. Imagine a teenager who reluctantly contacts friends, instead of the typical one who spends as much time as possible on their phone! It was not until I was in my mid-twenties and a practicing nurse, which required professional phone conversations, that I began to relax and not experience anxiety while conversing on a telephone.

Embracing vs Rejecting the Journey

After learning about Reiki, I began to experiment with it, but only on the people I trusted to give me accurate and compassionate feedback. Particularly, these were the nurses and surgeons in the operating room. Ever the skeptic but anxious to try the energy practice, I shared my desire to help anyone interested. One nurse who suffered from frequent headaches was my first willing candidate. I set my intention to bring Reiki through me to her as I placed a hand on each side of her head over her ears. After a few minutes, she expressed the headache had stopped.

On another day I was assigned to cover lunches in an operating room where this same nurse was in the first assistant role for a breast reduction surgery. I had relieved the circulating nurse, a role that remained unsterile and provided supplies or instrumentation to those scrubbed into the sterile surgical field. The plastic surgeon had a practice of using a suture once, requiring re-supply of the product fairly frequently during the procedure.

When the nurse with whom I had previously channeled energy saw me enter the room, she asked me to help her with a headache. After getting the hand-off of care report and making sure the scrub nurse had what she needed I walked up behind the assistant and put a hand over her ears on each side of her head. The surgeon looked up and asked what I was doing, and she explained that I was helping her get rid of a headache. He said he was the one that needed help and asked me to come over to his side of the table, complaining of a sore upper back. This was a great opportunity to test the process. I walked around the table and placed my hands just below his shoulders. He commented my hands were unusually hot, and I explained that I had been taught the heat was energy that would make him feel better. I wasn't sure it would work, as I was always "sure" it wouldn't work each time I attempted it, but it did. How, I did not know.

Anyway, as I stood hands resting on the surgeon's back, the scrub nurse ran out of the suture he was using, and he asked where the circulator went. I started to step away to get what he needed, and the surgeon told me to stay where I was and not take my hands off his back. He would use whatever the scrub nurse had available. His reaction strengthened my faith in energy practice.

After moving from Ohio to Virginia, I continued to help nurses and doctors I worked with, and eventually doctors asked if I would help their patients. They weren't sure it would help, but on occasion, when they had a critical patient, they wanted every opportunity available to help the patient through the surgical procedure. The more I practiced, the better outcomes I had.

I also benefitted. I would place my hand on a cut or scrape, and it would heal incredibly fast. Once a big piece of hospital machinery hit me right in the middle of my forehead, as witnessed by others in the room, but I did not have even a red mark on my skin at the point of contact. It was crazy, but it happened.

Another time I relieved the circulating nurse in a cardiac room just as the case finished. The patient began to exhibit unstable vital signs, and while the anesthesia team worked, and the surgeon remained, I offered to put my hands on the patient's chest and they agreed that it couldn't hurt. I did and the patient stabilized.

Unfortunately, at the turn of the century in a conservative southern culture, people began to look at me differently, wondering just who I was and where the healing ability came from. Some with strong religious beliefs began to gossip that it was the Devil's work, but I knew it wasn't. All I had done was use energy healing to help people feel better; I never asked for money with the practice, always freely volunteering my help.

While my energy healing abilities increased so did my sensitivity to bad human behavior. Prior to learning Reiki healing, I rarely cried, although I had always been very empathetic to others. But now I would often cry when I watched the news or witnessed acts of cruelty. It seemed to me that as my spiritual awareness grew my ability to protect my emotional self diminished. I began to understand why monks and nuns and other religious persons choose to isolate themselves from the rest of humanity.

Practice Experience

After receiving the Reiki I, II & Master certifications, I spent years helping others when the opportunity presented. I always considered myself an acute energy healer because I did not have a traditional practice of bringing people into a prepared setting and spending 40 minutes on a session. Those I helped were co-workers and patients in a variety of hospitals where I worked, and others I met socially who requested my help after the conversation turned to energy healing.

In all of those environments, I would begin by sharing that energy practice was of the spirit. I had to make sure a client understood there was no guarantee of success. Because I could not guarantee an outcome, I did not feel comfortable charging nor accepting a fee for my service, so I gave it away free to those I attempted to help. I believe that the spirit always determines what the body will receive. The spirit may disallow energy healing, even in a patient desiring it with complete sincerity.

While most minds think they lead the spirit through the body, the fact is that the Spirit leads the Mind through the Body.

SoZoKi is attaching to Spirit for energy to be guided through the body. We use our conscious Mind to set our intention to do so.

I successfully treated small complaints like sore necks, shoulders, knees, ankles, and backs, headaches, vertigo, and symptoms from chemotherapy. For those with advanced disease or terminal illness, I was able to provide comfort, helping them achieve acceptance while providing some relief from their physical and emotional discomfort. I always urged those I helped to continue their relationships with doctors, therapists, and pharmacists because energy healing should always be used as a complementary practice to Western medicine. (The same goes for all other alternative opportunities reviewed in Chapter 6). Energy practice is not for those whose ego needs to be fed. The practitioner is someone who opens themselves to serve as a vehicle for universal Reiki energy. They set an intention to bring energy into their own ethereal body so they can then deliver it to the ethereal body of the client. The energy is not the practitioner's own and the practitioner is not anointed by the Divine.

Later, I worked with a group of chronic pain patients who were referred by the Research Park at the University of Virginia. In 2009 the department had early insight into the long-term effects of opioid therapy and sought complementary opportunities for their patients. One of the pain clinic RNs reached out to see if I would participate in their effort. I agreed and began with a preliminary presentation to a group of pain patients who had signed up to learn and possibly participate. Six of the patients were interested enough to continue with sessions.

The first time I met with each of them I devoted more than an hour to a discussion of their pain experience. As a nurse, I wanted to know more about the specifics of their injury and as a Reiki Master, I wanted to know more about the circumstances surrounding it. During the consultation, when I felt they would benefit, I offered information on a variety of self-help practices including color and aroma therapy, nutrition, posturing practices, suggested books and articles, meditation, hydrotherapy, and shared personal experiences. After the consultation every return visit included a 45- to 60-minute energy session. I used my massage table and ensured they were as comfortable as possible before beginning to open their chakras to focus on specific issues.

Each person had their own experiences to relate at first, and all fell asleep during their sessions.

Once asleep they all exhibited one additional similar behavior: their abdomens would growl, that rumbling noise often attributed to being hungry. This would occur as I moved my hands over the solar plexus, just below the rib cage and above the navel. The solar plexus is the chakra of judgment or opinion, and I believe it was signifying their acceptance of self-identity as a pain patient, no longer the individual they had been before chronic pain entered their life. All commented as well, as to how the intense heat from my hands provided pain relief in varying degrees. One described my aura brilliantly colored before closing his eyes and dropping into a peace-filled energy state.

When we are told something repeatedly by a doctor or therapist, when we tell ourselves the same thing we are hearing, we tend to experience the idea as reality. I discovered over time that despite the help I was able to offer people in the moment, they generally did not let go of their identity as a chronic pain patient. It was as if they subconsciously embraced the label and were resigned to the consequences.

For those who would help others, I would warn them to avoid false expectations about what you might succeed in doing for others or for yourself. But do not lose faith in your insight and your ability when it comes to developing your self- energy practice.

8 - SoZoKi and Chakras

Surrounding and pervading the human body is the ethereal energy essence. It is energy layered close to the physical body that creates the human aura. Internally, energy is moved through swirling conical vortexes. These energy wheels are called *chakras*. You've probably heard the term, but it is important that you understand what they are, how they function, and what they mean to your well-being.

There are seven major chakras, each located where energy meridians or highways of the human body cross 21 times. Energy highways cross many times throughout the body, and it is those areas with a high volume of crossings that create the seven named major chakras. The first chakra is situated just below the perineum, the area between the legs where they join the torso. The seventh is located just above the crown head. In between lie the second through the sixth, actually within the physical body. (There are additional minor chakras that cross throughout the body, but we will discuss here only the seven major ones).

The chakras are best understood as a multi-dimensional system, and the interconnectedness of this system is an essential part of its nature. Each chakra – each energy vortex – supplies energy to the anatomical organs. When healthy and functioning without blocks, the chakras also promote inspiration and intuition, and influence judgments and opinions. What we communicate to others, how we perceive our place in Creation, and our attunement to spirit or soul consciousness are all colored by the vitality of our chakras. Our entire ethereal energy system is vitally integrated with our physiological organs and circulation. As you come to understand the functions of the chakras, you will see that each is identified with both traditionally feminine and masculine tendencies.

In my *Ésprit with SoZoKi* manual, a forthcoming teaching guide for new practitioners, I discuss each chakra, describing how it functions as a part of the whole, as well as ways to open chakras that are blocked and not fully functioning. I suggest reasons why a chakra might not be functioning to its fullest extent, and what the consequences can be. Diminished function of a chakra can not only decrease our vitality, but can impact our consciousness, our psyche, and the presence of disease in the physical body.

While I offer this information to assist you in safeguarding your spiritual and physical well-being, you must avail yourself of all care systems accessible, both Eastern and Western approaches to better health. You cannot throw either away when approaching a health issue. Never believe that you do not need to visit your medical (MD) or osteopathic (DO) doctor when you are suffering ill health. Failure to do so could jeopardize your well-being and diminish your ability to recover from injury or illness.

I cannot emphasize this enough: never throw either practice away. They work best in conjunction. If you are taking supplements, it is imperative to have a strong relationship with your pharmacist, as many non-medicinal supplements negatively react with, or negate the effectiveness of, prescribed Western medications. If you see a naturopath, you also need to see a medical doctor, physician's assistant, or nurse practitioner. If you see a chiropractor, it should be in conjunction with your primary care physician, and your orthopedic or neurosurgical specialist if you have been referred to one.

An exam is essential to ensure nothing is missed that could allow advancement of symptoms into an untreatable terminal condition or disease. Once cleared by an MD or DO you can seek the help of an alternative/supplemental provider and may not need to see the medical doctor again for the disorder. As a registered nurse, I must adamantly insist that this advice be taken by all who after reading this book seek to begin *Ésprit with SoZoKi* self-practice.

SoZoKi is the energy of life and all being.

SoZoKi is the foundation of everything, always and forever.

SoZoKi consoles and supports us in prayerful contemplation.

In a SoZoKi self-practice, we request energy from all of Creation – the Divine Design, God, E Pluribus Unum, the Universe – to enhance our own natural flow. There are many names for the fundamental name of the energy that is channeled in this practice. Whatever you think of as the source of all that is, understand that you don't have to give up your personal beliefs in the great power. A SoZoKi practice does not seek to replace any religious faith or non-theistic philosophy. You can be of any faith, or of none, and still draw on SoZoKi energy, and it is for this reason that even the skeptic can successfully receive and benefit from Creation's energy.

A fundamental ideological difference between the Reiki and SoZoKi systems of belief and practice is in the expectation of who will be the practitioner. Reiki is practiced solely by those attuned through ritual, under the guidance of a Reiki Master, to access the limited universe energy (Reiki). SoZoKi, on the other hand, teaches that anyone with awareness and desire to do so can access unlimited Creation energy. This is the natural path of energy flow; it is our connection to spirit or soul. Not at the behest of an anointed human. There is no one to give us permission or access.

SoZoKi sustains all life on earth be it plant, animal, or human and without our having to ask. SoZoKi is not a conscious effort to pull Earth or Universe energy but rather a practice to support a continuous subconscious flow of energy into our ethereal being. While this naturally occurring energy flow can be subconsciously diminished or blocked, it can also consciously be requested to increase. Energy condensing to form matter so that our spirit can have this earthly experience gives birth to the concept that human life is the process of evolution from human to spiritual consciousness.

9 - The Chakras

Root Chakra (First)

The first chakra is known as the Root. Located just below the perineum, the space between the anus and genitals, it connects to the coccyx, the lowest bone in the spine. It is primarily through this chakra that energy enters the human body's ethereal system. In the practice of Reiki, energy is drawn from the bio-magnetic field of the Earth and the universe beyond, while SoZoKi utilizes all energy that exists in Creation.

The prime functions of the Root Chakra are grounding, security, and survival. When the Root is closed, we shut ourselves off from inspired thought, and experience fear, anxiety, and depression. We can easily see the impact of a closed Root Chakra in our country. Americans have a high rate of occurrence of infertility, elimination complications (e.g., constipation), and psycho-social disorders. The prevalence of a dog-eat-dog mentality in a concrete jungle is evidence of a society suffering from a dis-attachment to spirit and the life energy flow of SoZoKi.

It is through the Root Chakra that inspired thought enters into our human consciousness, rather than the popular belief of initiation by way of the brain.

Sacral Chakra (Second)

The second energy vortex is known as the Sacral Chakra. It is located below the navel at the level of the bladder. As energy flows up from the Root, we experience intuition in the Sacral Chakra. When we are receptive to this intuition it is conceptualized into an idea. When our Sacral Chakra is blocked or inhibited, we reject intuition, losing the opportunity to experience inspired insight. The internal organs associated with this chakra experience failure, dysfunction, and/or disease. When we reject intuited ideas and deny non-rational knowledge, we have ultimately rejected the natural flow of SoZoKi.

The primary function of the Sacral Chakra is the governance of relationships and emotions. Expression of the sexual and intimate aspects of our nature is attached to the energy of this vortex. When the chakra is open and energy is flowing freely, we experience intuitive understanding in our intimate relationships. We know that we are loved and have no need for constant reassurance. We are inspired by this love. We understand that freedom to individuate in a partnership results in a relationship unencumbered by fear of loss resulting in one of the highest expressions of a healthy Sacral Chakra. When this chakra is open and flowing, we are sensitive in our relationships. We easily give and with equal ease receive, responding to the needs and gifts of those who share our life.

This chakra is also associated with our creative life. When it is healthy, we have a sense of "feeling alive," and creativity flows. When blocked, we experience frustration in our creative process or even lose the ability to be creative. Creativity is not limited to art forms but figures also in everything from business ventures to lifestyle choices. When this chakra is blocked it can manifest as illness, depleting or depressing our natural immune response.

A closed Sacral Chakra results in a loss of access to our intuitive process. In Western culture, intuition is pitted against a patriarchal, yang approach to life and the belief that a person experiences only that which can be objectively measured. Both men and women have often interpreted the feminine as hysterical in nature, and intuitive thought as flights of fantasy lacking verifiable data to substantiate the experience. But denying our intuition in turn dampens our creative flow. Subjective well-being has been studied by psychologists along with strategies to cope with mood. Thoughts of hopelessness enter our psyche and manifest as anxiety in Western cultures and clinical depression in Eastern cultures.

Solar Plexus Chakra (Third)

The third energy vortex is identified as the Solar Plexus Chakra and is located just above the umbilicus, also known as the navel or bellybutton. As inspiration and intuition flow through the first and second chakras, they arrive in the Solar Plexus where judgments or opinions are formed. When it is open, we accept the information provided by the Root and Sacral Chakras with positivity and grow the seed with integrated understanding. When this chakra is inhibited or closed, we dismiss those insights as insignificant or misguided, and we lose our intuition or gut feeling.

The prime function of the Solar Plexus Chakra is coordinating energy, vitality, and will power with our desires, and it is considered our body's battery. When energy flows freely through this chakra we have a sense of purpose, our state of mind is energized, and we experience our own autonomy.

The divine principle of this chakra is inner strength. With self-control we are efficient, pay attention to details and achieve the best results from the effort we apply. We need this vortex to function for when it does not, we fall victim to selfishness. When it is obstructed, we lack personal authority, and we seek power through the control of others rather than through self-control. Characteristic behaviors from aloofness to intimidation emerge to seek and draw energy from those with whom we interact. We fall victim to anger, fail at goals, and have a sense of purposeless existence.

(NB: After 25 years as an operating room nurse and having interviewed tens of thousands of patients, I am intrigued by the number of people in the U.S. who have reported they suffer from gastroesophageal reflux disease (GERD). In a Digestive Diseases and Science research article published on NCBI in 2014, the authors noted a steady rise in the rate of occurrence around the globe in industrialized countries. Annually more than 9 million visits to primary care doctors include complaints of GERD. GERD leads to utilization of sick leave which poses a financial burden on both the patients and their employers, and it also imposes a financial burden on health care systems. How many medications have been developed to stop acid in the stomach from rising up into the esophagus with a burning sensation often mimicking a heart attack? Television commercials are relentless, identifying the cause as a physical ailment to be treated with medication but not exploring the connections to our spiritual state of health. And now the discovery that some of those medications cause gastric cancer. GERD is the symptom, but is it a consequence of anatomical or ethereal dis-ease? Does constant judging produce GERD? We need to look for both pathologies in order to find lasting relief.

Reducing stress in our lives would certainly reduce GERD-related problems. We might start by cutting down on the number of judgements we make about ourselves as well as other people. There is no benefit in making judgment, only the ever-mounting cost of negativity and pain to our deeper selves.

Heart Chakra (Fourth)

The fourth energy vortex resides in the center of the chest and is known as the Heart Chakra. As energy flows into this chakra from the Solar Plexus, the rising judgment or opinion on the intuition and inspiration is given a second chance, re-consideration occurs, and opportunity for change emerges. When the flow of energy through this vortex is diminished or blocked, we miss the chance to replace dark thoughts with positive thoughts or intentions.

The prime function of the Heart Chakra is balanced love and connection. As the center of love for self, others and the Divine, it provides emotional equilibrium. It is also where ego resides and hope springs eternal. When this energy vortex is blocked or diminished, we lose our ability to be flexible, and hold only to rigid beliefs and behaviors. Our coping abilities decline. Feelings of trust and the impulse to share go missing, inhibiting our ability to love or be loved, and organs and body systems may exhibit disease or even failure. When open, energy flows to and through this chakra, and we experience compassion for ourselves and others, and are lifted by a positive attitude. Hope resides in the forefront of our thought processes. The Divine principles or goals of this chakra include forgiveness, sharing, respect, and openness to one another and to circumstance.

Throat Chakra (Fifth)

The fifth energy vortex, known as the Throat Chakra, is located mid-neck. As energy has risen through the preceding chakras, inspiration and intuition that was integrated in the first three vortexes, with the opportunity to be transformed in the fourth or Heart Chakra, reaches the throat and gives rise to what we communicate to the world.

When the chakra system is open, and the Heart Chakra is fully functional, we have the capacity to produce positive communication. When closed or dysfunctional, our vocalizations become negative, seeking to denounce or denigrate rather than lift or elevate those with whom we interact. While Creation Energy always flows from a source that is positive in charge, impaired lower chakras can twist the intent. Evil can be described as bad decisions made by our conscious, human mind, and we must acknowledge and accept responsibility for our own behavior rather than fall prey to the tendency to blame an external evil which "forced" poor decision-making upon us, denying our freewill ("The devil made me do it").

This chakra's prime functions are communication and healing. Our creative process is also aligned here, and it is this vortex that provides the ability to see others as whole individuals and acknowledge the One Will of the Creator. The energy of language is filled with powerful words having the ability to heal and lift higher, but also can humiliate, harm, hinder, or humble. As we interact with others, it is through this chakra that we can stimulate goodness, convey appreciation, and respect, or offer comfort, but it can also be the means to disparage and degrade. Speech can be used to "divide and conquer," or fracture unity through criticism, defamation, and divisiveness.

Third Eye Chakra (Sixth)

The sixth energy vortex is known as the Third Eye and is located above the eyebrows in the middle of the forehead. It is thought to be connected to the brain. Prior to energy flowing into this chakra from the throat, inspiration, intuition, judgment, re-evaluation, and communication have all taken place. In this chakra we arrive at an understanding of our place in Creation. When we acknowledge the pattern and flow of energy that occurred in the first five chakras, we find ourselves able to accept that we are united with all that exists, neither above nor below, nor separate in any way from all else. It is because of this the Third Eye is considered the seat of our celestial body.

It is within the Third Eye that imagination emerges and where we open our spirit fully to SoZoKi. When energy is blocked or diminished, we may find it difficult to learn new skills. Our memory and pattern recognition, which are the bases of our ability to classify data and experience, may be impaired. The prime function of the Third Eye is integration and understanding. It is through this vortex that we see beyond the five physiological senses of our anatomical body: sight, hearing, touch, taste, and smell. The Third Eye Chakra is considered the center of clairvoyance. It is here that we have our sixth sense, our psychic ability; it is the sense that resides within our celestial rather than physical body. The Divine principle of this chakra is the use of imagination and clairvoyance to see our spirit as it relates to all Creation.

Crown Chakra (Seventh)

The seventh energy vortex, which completes the major chakra system, is known as the Crown, the center of enlightenment. Just as the Root Chakra is below what is often identified as the trunk of our body, the Crown swirls above the top of our head. This chakra has an exogenous property, meaning it is derived from a source outside of an organism. As with the Root Chakra, the lines of meridian cross 21 times outside of our physical body to create the Crown Chakra. While the Root provides positive SoZoKi that fires up our energy system, it is the exogenous nature of the Crown Chakra that sustains both our physical and ethereal bodies.

The Third Eye focuses on our place in creation, but it is the Crown that attaches us to SoZoKi and maintains flow when centers are open and functioning freely. As energy exits the Crown it circles back to the Root in a continuous cycle of spirit and sense. Even though we may not understand, or even be aware of, this energy system, our acceptance of "something greater than our self" is essential.

It is with a well-developed and high-functioning Crown Chakra that our spirit rises above human consciousness, and the life stories we have told ourselves fade away to be replaced with self-actualization. Does this mean we will no longer experience pain, suffering or loneliness? No, it does not. What it does mean is the self-centered idea of being - that we are only accountable for those in our family, tribe or religious communities - fades, and we come to understand that while our spirit may be housed in an individual body/mind, it is a part of something far larger and greater...and that larger reality is all we know and all there is yet to know.

The prime function of the Crown energy vortex is enlightenment and transcendence. Spiritual understanding gives way to spirit consciousness. The Divine principle is divinity in the company of higher values and wisdom. Inspiration, higher reason, and awareness are the goals associated with the Divine's SoZoKi.

Life is filled with rhythms: tide, moon, season, sleep, and reproduction cycles are a few that readily come to mind. While the natural world adheres to these cycles, day in and day out, month in and month out, year in and year out, we humans seem intent on finding ways to regulate reproduction and sleep. We use a variety of birth control measures to stop our reproductive cycles. We work at night and sleep during the day. We may need seven to eight hours of sleep every twenty-four hours, but many Westerners are sleep deprived. Busy minds inhibit the activity of the pineal hormones and in particular its production of melatonin, the chemical messenger that allows us to naturally fall easily into sleep each night.

As an operating room nurse I have witnessed, again and again, families keeping loved ones alive past their natural life cycle, often putting them through horrific medical procedures, because they can't let them go naturally back to the Divine and complete the bodily cycle of life.

As I participated in surgical procedures in 23 hospitals in 23 cities in 11 states across the USA, one theme became apparent to me. When it is time for our Spirit to leave this life, it is time. No matter the intervention or lack thereof, it is the Spirit attached to the Divine that ends the life of the physical body.

10 - *Ésprit with SoZoKi Self-Practice*

*Allow Creation's Energy to Manifest and
Sustain Light, Love and Truth in My Life
Today and Every Day*

<u>Starting & Ending Each Day</u>

Is it your morning ritual to sleep as long as possible before rising into a maelstrom of activity – household chores, work, or appointments? Parents command the routines that send pets outside and children off to school. Most of us want to approach the day with a clean face, appropriately dressed. All of this stimulation focuses our thoughts on rising onto tasks to be accomplished and anticipated challenges of the coming day. If possible, it is healthier to take time to greet the day with gratitude and wonder before setting your course.

I do my best to ensure I do not have to get up and rush to meet my day. I prefer to take my time, going to bed early if necessary, so that when I wake I can pet my dogs, drink my coffee, and then exercise if I feel like it, listen to some music, or check the news of the day. Sometimes I turn on an entertaining television show, but then again, I might just sit quietly to hear a bird sing a song. I don't rush through a shower, throw on clothes and run to work. While I have something of a routine, I try not to be rigid about it, mixing it up a bit so that I enjoy the start of each day as new and different. Routines are efficient but it can also be tedious to follow the same steps each morning, day in and day out.

A friend believes there is also something to be said for creating a foundation for your day by making your bed before facing the world. Eh, I pull up the covers but there is no official "making" of the bed.

I often slow and set the pace of my gate as I exit my car and walk into the building. I do this to set my pace for the day. I don't do it every day but I always do it when work is excessively demanding.

When we run after anything we are reacting and have lost the opportunity to intentionally act upon. When we run we have succumbed to a reactionary life that is lived in response to an event rather than with purpose.

Not everyone is able to control our schedules to this extent, and I realize this is easy for me to say because I am able to a large extent. But planning a calm moment before heading into the day is worth some effort to arrange. Particularly if you are the sort of person who wakes with dread, give yourself a way to turn that negativity around. It may be that you write a positive statement on a post-it note and stick it to your bathroom mirror. If you are a sleepyhead, you might play music that is upbeat and makes you want to continue listening instead of falling back to sleep. Most importantly, make sure you do get enough sleep!

Getting enough sleep is easier said than done if you find it challenging to easily fall asleep to begin with. The good news is there is a variety of ways to help the process. First, stop stimulating yourself a couple of hours before you head to bed. No news on the television, no talk radio, no action movies or horror shows – that goes for reading as well – and no screen time in general. Some people readily fall asleep after reading one or two pages, but others, once they have started reading, find themselves lost in a book for hours. Before they know it only a few hours are left to sleep before the start of the new day. Beware! A tired person is an unhappy person, and unhappy people unwittingly invite negative encounters with others.

On those occasions when I want to go to sleep – or back to sleep – but my mind won't stop its restless activity, I turn to New Age music and energy channeling. As I move my hands through the Reiki energy positions, I rarely get past my heart before falling into a deep sleep. Other opportunities to calm your mind include meditation, yoga, breathing the scent of lavender and drinking chamomile tea. Calm your mind. Allow a pause in your stream of thoughts so that sleep finds its way to you.

Fresh New Beginnings

Can you feel the earth move, sense a low vibration?
Wheels on a distant road rushing to a new location?
When you look up at the clouds, what is it you see?
White on a blue canvas - images appear to me.

What do you hear when a bird sings his song?
He will carry a melody, if you listen well and long.
As you first awake, what is it you feel?
Fresh, as-yet unburdened? Can that peace be real?

A fresh new beginning is found in each sunrise
Yesterday has past, will you let this day surprise?
Look at yourself, the one you know, the 'you' down
deep inside
Hold that image in your mind, as each moment in
life glides

To weave a unique story, the one that is called your
life
When you advocate for love, your endeavor serves
to replace strife
With love that finds its way to heart and then into
your mind
You will find your spirit at play, releasing what life
has confined

So, find peace within each day, it's something we all
possess!
Believe in purpose for your life, and try to not always test

Your faith in the Creator, who dwells in each of us
For life will quicken before our eyes as the body
returns to dust.

03.15.2001 / 09.04.2018 / 11.15.2020

Creating Your Space

Some may call it creating an altar, you may call it
designing your intentional-thought-and-behavior
place – it does not matter what you call the space
you make, it is only important that you create it.
Consider what and when use of it will occur and
who will participate. When the goal is to change
one's world perspective from half-empty to half-
full, and one's behaviors from health-degrading to
vitality-building, time spent planning sustainable
practice is worthwhile.

Planning, practice, and time. Yes, it takes time to
turn a habit of negativity into a consistently positive
life practice. Think about how long you may have
been approaching life with pessimism. Did it begin
during your childhood or adolescence? Does it date
back to being a young adult? Older adult? The longer you have been harboring negativity the more
effort you need to put into planning for change. It is
essential that you are honest with yourself! You,
and only you, know every little weakness you possess, and you need to own them all, each and every
one.

Make sure you freely speak to each item in the space. You must consider everything from the floor up. Include space for a yoga mat, comfortable chair or beanbag, and multiple seating possibilities. Consider lighting, ventilation, and audio capability. Plan for the types of hydration you will want (water, tea, electrolyte drinks) and how you will provide aromatherapy (candles, incense, vaporizer, atomizer). Choose any religious talismans important to your spiritual beliefs. You may also want to light a candle of a chakra color, burn incense to cleanse an energy center, listen to music, and/or follow yoga posing, in a very cold, very hot, or breezy atmosphere. Work with what you have; don't allow your current environment to act as limitations to success. A separate room may not be feasible, but a corner can suffice. An altar can be tiny, up high on a shelf, or tucked into a cupboard. There are many possibilities. It's the connection between you and who you are that matters. In my mother's words, "Don't be your own worst enemy, Nancy – can't never could!"

As you return over the course of time to this sacred space you have created, as you practice meditation, self-healing or healing of another, your ability to access positive energy and your ability to increase flow to improve health will grow. Use the Reiki symbols, readily found online, visualizing them at the start of your meditation practice, or place them in the form of art on the walls or in picture-frames on tables and shelves. Create an *intention board* – where you list your goals – with repetitive, inspiring words or pictures of places, spaces, and people who are meaningful to you, while concentrating on what you wish to manifest in your life. Define your mantra, your desires, your promise to self to remain on this path. Begin and end each session with gratitude and thanks for the opportunity to commune your Holy Spirit and the Divine, with SoZoKi.

Define Your Rituals

For every aspect of life, be it religion or culture, education, athletics or military, all societies make use of ritual. Ritual is used to provide relief through prayer, to maintain and sustain a community and to impart knowledge and see that it passes down through the generations. Rituals are present in celebrations, inductions, memorials and to commemorate passages throughout life, from birth to death, marking our existence with words, gestures, and manipulation of objects in repetitive sequences. Rituals can be personal or communal, serving to promote a feeling of protection or enable harm.

In your practice of *Ésprit with SoZoKi* you will need to create rituals as you develop your self-energy practice. To help you get started, I ask that you set this book aside after reading this section and have pencil and paper at hand. I suggest you put yourself on a timer so that you don't lose an afternoon unintentionally! Limit this kind of time to an hour of your day to begin with.

Consider what is included in rituals. We eat and drink, sleep, exercise the body/brain – we work, play, have sex, give birth, and create. Very importantly, we also think. We are constantly filtering a barrage of data points and monitoring seemingly endless variables, while trying to maintain course and speed and a sense of balance. Your energy practice rituals should touch on each of these aspects of your life. You may choose to achieve this throughout the day at different opportunities or to practice at one set, recurring time.

If you are a negative thinker, begin where your thoughts flow naturally, setting down on that piece of paper in front of you whatever comes to mind. Do phrases usually start with something like "I can't" or "I don't "? "They won't" or "they shouldn't"? Any of those sounding familiar? Make a list on paper of those and similar comments that you say or think, but make sure you leave a space next to each phrase, because you are going to want to painstakingly rewrite those negative statements to read – and implant in your heart and mind – "I can," "I do," "they may" or "they shall."

The degree of your attachment to your usual monologue will dictate the amount of time you spend with this daily ritual. I suggest you do this several times a day, and that you limit the number of phrases; say to six. Just as it takes a few times to get the hang of almost everything we learn to do, we need to accommodate ourselves when we are learning to observe, with the intention of changing, our thoughts. Eventually you can choose a time, at the ending of your day if the mornings are too rushed, to do this practice.

Sleep is an important ritual, and adequate sleep is one of the most beneficial health habits you can cultivate. Everyone requires a different amount, but most need somewhere between seven and eight hours each night. A rare few only need four hours to maintain their emotional and physical health. But for most of us, such little sleep is detrimental. I'm an eight-hour person, and while I function fine on seven, by the end of a week I can tell a difference in my energy level simply from missing one hour of sleep a night. While naps are good, they don't compensate for missed sleep. We cannot "catch up" on sleep – we either get it or we don't; the consequences ensue, and weekends spent sleeping hardly correct the harm done during the week.

In virtually all faith practices, the existence of sexual energy is acknowledged, and yet this energy is often simultaneously denied. What happens when natural sexual energy is not released? Frustration, which can lead to depression, angry outbursts, poor eating habits, low self-esteem, lack of vitality, and, not least, an inability to establish healthy sleep hab-

its. These are just a few potential consequences.
Lust and the drive to reproduce are not necessarily
expressions of the emotion we call love, but mind-
fully integrating these desires into our lives is essential to our well-being just the same. Hormones,
which are tied to gender and genetics, play a powerful role in our physical body, but they also play a
powerful role in our emotions, resulting in decisions that produce or withhold actions.

Work: how is that going for you? Most of us must
do it! If to meet your basic needs you experience
physical distress due to suppressed or unconscious
dislike for your job and/or your boss, think about
alternatives. If you are disappointed with co-workers or your career trajectory, find a way to make
changes. Yes, "God helps those who help themselves," is easier said than done, but "doing" as
opposed to just "trying" is at the root of this bit of
wisdom about making change.

As you explore these aspects in your life, your
energy-healing abilities for self and others will
grow. They will blossom. Again, change does not
occur overnight. You will need to develop and accept an honest self-evaluation. The good news is
that only you, with your spiritual consciousness, are
involved in this process. You do not need an appointment for therapy or need to attend an organized group for support. You can continue your
religious practice; attend classes that stimulate your

mind or body; join programs that provide volunteer services – but while you continue with all of these be sure to begin your personal energy-healing practice, nurturing your lively spirit. And if your schedule seems too filled, you might consider focusing on your own true needs before acting on those of others.

Successful Meditation

In the final chapter I have provided a non-guided meditation for those who have encountered difficulty with calming the mind, preventing or inhibiting a successful self-practice. Often our minds are overflowing with the details we continuously consider as we live each day. It is said that we have 60,000 thoughts a day. Attempting to calm this process can be very difficult. Frustration can result in abandoning the practice of meditation altogether.

I would recommend experimenting with the non-guided meditation if you have been unable to practice with previous methods. Chapter Six identifies the benefits of meditation, and the Notes section at the end of this book offers multiple references to explore as you start and then broaden your meditation practice. You may think you do not have the time to include a daily practice of meditation! But I ask that you think again. You do not have to be in a special place, and you don't need to secure a large amount of time to incorporate this way of increasing your energy flow into your life. At the outset calming your mind may take much of the time you have set aside, but after you have developed your approach you will find yourself transitioning into a meditative state more readily. In time you will be able to identify the time of day when meditation is most feasible. You should also be able to identify experiences that would benefit from brief meditative moments, for example before embarking on a complex task or addressing a difficult topic with others.

Meditation is an opportunity to remind yourself of your own spiritual consciousness. It is an opportunity to connect with the Divine and access SoZoKi to grow your awareness of the opportunities that exist throughout your day. Like prayer, meditation is a powerful process, bringing love and respect to yourself so that you can then shower it upon others in your life.

Reinforce Patterns

Understanding and identifying daily mantras to assist you in staying connected to your spirit is imperative to successful evolution of your thoughts and actions. What are your mantras? More fundamentally, what is a mantra? And how do we identify ones that speak to us? Mantra is a word taken from Hindi with origins in the part of the Vedas containing hymns. Originally used to denote repetitive phrases from sacred texts, or special words used to incite charms or spells, in 1956 the word *mantra* was introduced into the English language to describe an instrument of thought, or more specifically, an instrument to help us control our thoughts. Mantras can also be the vocalizations of a sound or series of words repeated during meditative practice to calm the flood of thoughts that engage our mind every day.

Most of us in the West don't live in a social environment that would support meditation breaks throughout the course of a day. Sustained attention to the nurturance of the spirit simply is not featured in our capitalist society. The minimal, and legally mandated, breaks given to the workforce focused on food, drink, and usage of restroom facilities are provided to enhance worker productivity, and not necessarily out of concern for workers' spiritual health.

What is spiritual health? While it is intrinsically difficult to define, we can observe the outcomes of healthy spirit in improved emotional, social, and physiological states. Our ability to achieve communal harmony with all life is possible but requires a little more effort on the part of the everyday American. Many cultures around the world are far more advanced in spiritual pursuits than ours is in the United States. American faith traditions tend to lean towards spiritual practice gatherings on the particular sabbath and less so during the week.

Dealing with the Caustic

We need nourishment for the body but give limited time to feeding the spirit. We can develop our mantras and learn to weave them throughout our day into our conscious thoughts to nurture our souls. The application of this approach will help you in the day-to-day. You don't have to fall victim to negative behavior patterns of a co-worker. You may start your day out feeling great but arrive at the office only to encounter a stream of complaints from your boss, an associate, or a client. But your day doesn't have to go downhill from there. What to do?

First you must identify the patterns. You awoke rested, you enjoyed your morning, your thoughts were forward-looking – and then another person brought you down into the gloomy reality they have created for themselves. This is exactly when your self-energy practice of *Ésprit with SoZoKi* will help you survive or even uplift this interaction. Your mantra should be accessible – perhaps you can read it upon arrival at your desk, a reminder to self to stop the craziness before it starts. Silently repeat your mantra to drown out the tirade you know is coming. Offer a short and to-the-point statement of concern (I'm sorry you're struggling with/ frustrated by/ unhappy about x"), followed up immediately with "There is a work issue that was on my mind all night on which I need to focus my attention." Most importantly, do not apologize! "I wish I could" or "I'm sorry not now" leaves the door wide open for a "Next time"!

Self-preservation necessitates recognition of those moments when another's compelling need to feel empowered dominates and calls for civil but firm disengagement. Deny someone the opportunity to feed on your attention at will, and you will free yourself to align your own spirit where you will. If you wish to sacrifice yourself to their hunger then by all means do so, but understand that to empower yourself you must own your own behavior and set your own spiritual course.

So you reach for a mantra, you remind yourself of the value of those words in the moment, and finally you carry out an action plan that deflects attempts to pull you down while it enhances your own connection with spirit. Touché...We're done...You can do this!

Inviting Energy of the Spirit

Begin by "setting your intention," in other words, directing your thoughts and intentions towards your desired result. This can take the form of a prayer, recited in your mind or aloud. As I described in Chapter 6, a shaman prayer used by a massage therapist at the outset of a session channeled the same energy I had previously only associated with Reiki practice. A clear vision with firm intention yields powerful results. Shamanism offers guidance in staying in the present as though your goal is already achieved. Pray from your heart with intense emotion to power your intention into reality. Precisely use the words you have chosen, make them clear and unequivocal. Affirm your trust in the Holy Spirit, leaving no room for doubt. Make use of the words "I am" and focus on a point within your heart. Rhyme, rhythm, and repetition can inspire and illuminate your prayer. Spend some time in quiet contemplation after you pray. Refrain from the urge to push or scrounge but listen for inspired thought. Finally, complete the meditation with an action in support of your desired outcome.

There exists a wide variety of approaches to prayer, some antagonistic. The way a person sees their world – including politics, culture, race, and creed – influences the way they pray. One may pray for an enemy to be killed, another may instead ask that they be forgiven or saved. Some pray for abundance, while still others become angry with the Divine because they feel powerless in a difficult life, or ignored in the face of their belief that they are known to God. Some are thankful, praising God for the love they feel, acknowledging how wonderful God is, and identifying themselves as a reflection of the Almighty, seeking God's will to be done.

If you prefer a prayer that has always held significance in your life, then recite it. I also recommend that you spend some time on a Google search seeking positive statements that ring true to you.

Feet and Hand Chakras

There are 122 minor chakras throughout the body, and each bears many of the same characteristics of the seven major chakras. Yes, energy can be seen in color. Red light has lower and blue light higher energy levels. Most, but not all of us, have the ability to see color. Just the opposite is true for the ability to see energy fields. Those with the ability to see auras, may also see chakras appearing as little cyclones, each a whirling energy vortex located in the body's joints. Examples include chakras within the hands and feet as well as those in the shoulders, elbows, wrists, hips, and knees. Minor chakras are also located where nerve plexuses or bundles exist throughout the body.

Dysfunction of the secondary chakras can have a detrimental impact on the entire chakra system. Connective tissue is primarily responsible for carrying electromagnetic energy and much of that tissue is located in our buttocks and legs. If the energy cycle is cut off below the hips, it reduces by almost 40 percent the natural energy that feeds our vital internal organs. The result can be diminished life force impairing our functioning every day.

In the U.S. we tend to identify ourselves as highly intellectual, giving importance to the upper part of our body over the lower part, often thinking we are a "cut above" those with lesser intellects. With this thought comes the potential to cut off energy flow in the legs resulting in dysfunction. Sluggish bodies and sleepy heads produce confusion, depression, and frustration with our inability to establish a balanced mind, body, and spirit.

If you have this approach to living you may not be able to use your feet to ground your spirit to the earth energies, and then guide it up your legs, through your hips and into your Root Chakra. To rethink the importance you have placed solely on superior intellect is to recognize the imbalance the whole world suffers when this idea reigns.

Foot chakras function primarily to bring energy into your ethereal body. Most guided meditations have you visualize growing roots from your foot chakras, filaments that extend past the floor of a room and down through the building, sending them deep into the earth to access abundant and available energy. In the SoZoKi meditation and self-practice, the foot chakras are used to ground spirit to earth energy lightly before sending it out to Creation. Roots emerge from the feet out across a large plot of earth, spreading shallowly instead of growing deeply. Energy is pulled from the Earth, but the majority of energy is brought in from infinite Creation rather than finite Earth.

NB: While the Root Chakra benefits from Earth energy pulled through foot chakras, the majority of energy entering the ethereal body via the Root is SoZoKi in a constant flow and is increased when our intention is set.

Hand chakras are associated with the upper three major chakras (Throat, Third Eye, and Crown). While filled with secondary chakras at the many joints, the hands have one larger vortex in the center of the palm. Because of the number of minor hand chakras, energy flow is not limited to the palm. Each finger transmits energy associated with colors. Red is traditionally channeled from the index finger and thumb (Root Chakra), green from the middle (Heart), blue from the ring finger (Throat) and violet from the pinky (Crown). The energy flow that produces the colors is influenced by the status of the upper chakras, as well as by physical limitations of the neck and shoulders. A stiff neck can reduce the energy in the hands as well as the colors emanating from the fingers.

Associated with acts of giving and receiving, the hand chakras are used to channel energy to heal another as well as bring energy for self-healing. Signs of healthy and open hand chakras include openness, confidence, and creativity. When you feel numb or closed off, when you experience a lack of creativity or are unable to express yourself artistically, or when you feel disconnected from those in your circle or the world at large, you may be experiencing symptoms of closed hand chakras or diminished entry of SoZoKi into your ethereal body. You likely will have difficulty in channeling to another, nor bringing energy in to heal yourself.

Not to worry! There are things you can do to help your hand chakras. Creating art is not limited to those with natural talent. Everywhere you look you can now find coloring books for adults, published in traditional paper and colored pencil format but also available in free electronic apps. Other opportunities would be to take a sculpting class or learn to throw clay. Or you may like working with wood, painting ceramic pieces, or creative cooking.

A self-healing practice of SoZoKi can also open your hand chakras. The more you practice the more they will open. Resting your hands in a bowl of water while you visualize the chakras open is another simple therapy readily available to most. One well-known Reiki practice is known as building *ki* or *chi*. Holding your hands with palms facing and 4-6 inches apart, close your eyes and bring your mind's focus to the space between your palms. To begin to build so that you can feel energy slowly bring your hands apart about an inch and then gently move them back. This back and forth motion will build the energy between your hands, helping to open the chakras. As your hands move in you begin to feel a light resistance, and as they move our you feel stretching.

Some practitioners recommend rubbing your palms together to open the chakras. I would suggest that if you do follow this guidance rubbing your hands should be a light touching for only a few moments. When you rub your hands vigorously, they may feel as though a heating pad has been placed on them due to the friction you have generated. This can provide a false sense of energy flow which is not therapeutic.

Hand Positions for Moving Energy

Self-healing hand positions always begin with focused intention using a prayer of your choice. You can sit, lie flat, or stand. Make yourself comfortable so that your focus can remain on energy movement rather than an uncomfortable position. Hand positions are always a light touch or hover, whichever is most comfortable. Typically, you will feel motivated to move to the next position after a few minutes.

To assist with sleep or target a specific chakra dysfunction, begin by placing the palm of each hand over right and left eyes. Next, move your cupped hands to hover over or lightly touch the right and left ears. Using the same light touch or hovering position, remain until you feel ready to move on with your healing, then place your hands on top or just above the crown of your head. The final position for the Third Eye and Crown Chakras is on the back of the head. This can be accomplished by reaching up and over your head, but for most it is more comfortable to place the hands from the right and left sides. It does not matter which hand is upper or lower.

Continuing downward you will move your hands so that the palms are placed gently over the anterior (front) side of the neck, below the chin and above the chest, to address the Throat Chakra. If you have a long neck you can place them individually with one upper and one lower. Those with a shorter neck may have to overlap them a bit to fit the space.

It is not recommended to place your hands together for the Heart Chakra, but rather to place the palm of each hand on your right and left chest above the nipple line (even though the chakra is located in the middle of the chest). Again, this is a light touch and your hands will remain still until you feel you should move.

Just below the breastbone and above the navel, place your hands palm down over the Solar Plexus, one above and one below and slightly lifted to face each other. Emphasis is a slight lift. The palms are not parallel to each other but remain mostly facing the chakra in a cupped position.

As you move your hands downward, you will place them palms down over the area where the Sacral

Chakra is located, below the navel and above the pubic bone, generally over the area where the bladder lies within the physical body. The angle of the hands remains the same as it was for the Solar Plexus. When ready you will then move your hands below the trunk of your body, between the top of the thighs, where the Root Chakra is located. Your hands will hover over this chakra rather than rest on the body. If your intention is to treat the entire chakra energy system, use the SoZoKi medication that starts with the root.

In the companion manual I provide detailed description for each of the chakras. As you move your hands through the positions, focus your attention on the function of each chakra. At each hand position, affirm your intention that SoZoKi enter the chakra, and then move from it to the associated supporting structures and organs. Visualize the color of each chakra, and in your mind's eye see the swirl of energy moving into and then out of the vortex.

You will not always have time or need to complete a full body energy session. Sometimes you may only want to focus on a particular spot, like a sore knee, hip, foot, elbow, or shoulder. Other times you may wish to use SoZoKi to help you stop your mind so that you can fall asleep. As mentioned before, I have great success playing soft meditation music while moving my hands through chakra positions. I typically am asleep by the time my hands have moved to my chest in the Heart Chakra position.

If you prefer a prayer that has always held significance in your life, then recite it. I again recommend that you spend some time on a Google search seeking positive statements that ring true to you. These varying approaches to prayer remind me of two models used in healthcare and beyond. The first is the Kubler-Ross model, introduced in the 1950s, and known as the five stages of grief. Initially introduced as the observed stages of a person diagnosed, or closely dealing, with a terminal illness, they include denial, anger, bargaining, depression, and acceptance.

The second model is Maslow's hierarchy of needs, introduced to the field of psychology in the 1940s. In this model, Maslow identified the stages of psychological growth. At the bottom of the pyramid, the base or foundation is to meet our physiological needs of homeostasis, food, water, sleep, and shelter. After this level has been met, our psychological focus is on safety and includes personal security, financial security, and health or well-being. Once satisfied we move upward to esteem, respect, self-confidence, strength, independence, and freedom, seeking sustenance for the ego through status and recognition. Next we reach for self-actualization, acquiring a mate, creating and parenting offspring, using our abilities and talents, pursuing goals, and seeking happiness. Finally we move beyond self-actualization into self-transcendence with the realization of a desire beyond self, becoming Creation's Energy altruistic spirit, relating to others humanely, as well as to other species and the environment.

NB: *As we move through life's stages, our access to Creation's Energy is enhanced by purposeful practice.*

Setting Your Intention

I refer again to Chapter Six, and earlier in this chapter, when I shared the story of the second massage therapist named Pat, who provided another significant insight. In Richmond, the first Pat shared Leslie's message, teaching me our spirit consciousness does survive the body. In Virginia Beach the second Pat, using a Shaman prayer to set his intention, taught me energy is energy.

NB: I bring this up again to share the following. On more than one occasion I have been asked to become someone's spiritual guide, and each time I have declined. My intention is to help you partner with your spirit, allowing it to guide your life.

11 - Ésprit Energy Meditations

Born in 1956, I grew into my adolescence in the late '60s, when Transcendental Meditation (TM) came onto the alternative healing scene. I was between two generations with widely differing world views, but I aligned myself with the hippie generation of love and peace in the pursuit of happiness rather than with elders who defined material acquisition as the essence of a successful life.

Although I had never practiced TM, during recovery from a physical assault in 2000, I found myself frequently gliding into meditative states as part of my healing process. As mentioned before, I was diagnosed with subluxation (a partial dislocation) of all cervical (neck) vertebrae, with a bulging and herniated disc in the direction of my spinal cord at two levels. I did not take a drug stronger than Aleve (an over-the-counter anti-inflammatory), but I visited a chiropractor five days a week for minimal mechanical manipulation of my cervical spine and application of a TENS unit (transcutaneous electrical nerve stimulation) to calm the injured muscles that were pulling my spine out of its natural alignment.

I was also under the care of a neurologist. Working in conjunction with the chiropractor and a physical therapist providing therapeutic massage, who saw to it that my neck mobility was maintained. I was offered the option of surgery but as an operating room nurse, I knew I would do whatever was necessary to prevent a surgical fusion of my neck. For five months I was confined to a chair while I waited for the symptoms to subside so I could begin a physical rehabilitation program.

As a practicing Reiki Master, each day I requested Creation's energy to enter my being and heal my body and the heartache that permeated my conscious mind. I would effortlessly fall into a theta, or subconscious, state. Time would pass with no retained memory. I had time enough on my hands while sitting in that chair, and time moves very slowly when you cannot fully engage life. Yet I received an amazing gift during my recovery. God's grace bestows gifts and mine was an explosion of artistic ability. Each day saw a significant improvement over the previous one, and today I share the collection of my first portraits whenever I feel it would benefit another in need after a tragic event, or others who are struggling to find meaning in their own traumatic life experiences.

During this time I also went far beyond the traditional Reiki work and spent almost two years exploring books on the subject of energy healing. Layering this information with my nursing knowledge, I began to understand the multi-disciplinary function of the ethereal energy system in and around our anatomic body.

Many if not most guided meditations I have participated in have been focused on grounding the listener to Earth energy. I see nothing wrong with this approach, but I believe it is essential to offer an additional mode to calm the mind while invoking Creation's love. The Earth offers incredible energy to support all that dwells on it. However, there exists much more than our little blue planet. Powerful as its energy is, it is a part of Creation, so why not reach beyond the limitations of Earth, beyond our solar system, beyond our universe and request the support of all of Creation? The following are two meditations designed to access Creation's limitless energy.

Non-Guided Meditation

For those who prefer a non-guided meditation I recommend the following, especially if you are a beginner or have had difficulty in the past in calming your mind. You will need the following: an unscented candle, a comfortable seating arrangement, turn the phone, television, and music off, ensure pets/family are in a part of your home where they will not interrupt you for at least 15 minutes and use a room that you can completely darken. The idea is to remove all external stimuli except the candle you will light.

Once you are comfortable, have lit the candle and removed all other stimuli you will begin a rolling breath technique. You many need to start at a slow count of 4 and work your way up to 8, or you might have great breathing already and can count to 8 without difficulty. The idea is to begin a slow inhale through your nose, filling the lower lobes of your lungs and then filling them to capacity. Just as you have reached capacity there is a very brief pause before you begin to exhale slowly through your mouth. If you have difficulty breathing through your nose don't worry, you can use only your mouth and still get the same outcome. Purposeful breathing is what you are trying to train yourself to do as we rarely think about breathing unless we can't do it.

If you can do no more than a count of 4 you will begin filling your lungs mentally counting to 4 and then count again to 4 on the exhale. At the end of inhale and exhale is a very brief pause. This is the rolling breath technique. Eventually with practice you will increase your capacity to 8 and will also no longer need to count as you have trained your body to the process.

After you have successfully created your breathing

technique you will then move your focus from your breathing to the flickering flame of the candle. You can practice this while you are in breath training so that when you no longer need to count you will be able to relax your mind. Allow the flame to transition your mind into what it referred to as a Beta Mind State or the subconscious overpowering the conscious mind.

The following guided mediation will be available on YouTube later in 2021 for those seeking an internally guided experience. Here I have provided the narrative and once learned you can use music and/or visual media to enhance the experience. Regardless of your approach it is always best that you are not going to be interrupted by life and you are in a very comfortable position and climate.

Guided Ésprit Meditation

Begin the *Ésprit with SoZoKi* meditation with 6 rolling breaths. Slowly begin inhaling through your nose, filling the lower lobes of your lungs. As the space is filled complete the inhale by filling your upper lungs to capacity. Briefly pause and begin to exhale through your mouth, slowly allowing the air to escape out of your upper lungs, then mildly push the remaining air out of your lower lungs. Breath in through your nose filling the lower and then upper lungs to capacity. After a brief pause, slowly exhale, allowing the air to escape out of your upper lungs, then mildly push the remaining air out of your lower lungs. Breath in through your nose filling the lower and then upper lungs to capacity. After a brief pause, slowly exhale, allowing the air to escape out of your upper lungs, then mildly push the remaining air out of your lower lungs. Breath in through your nose, filling the lower and then the upper lobes of the lungs to capacity. After a brief pause, slowly exhale, allowing the air to escape out of your upper lungs, then mildly push the remaining air out of your lower lungs. Again, breath in through your nose filling the lower lobes of your lungs and then upper lobes to capacity. Pause briefly and then slowly exhale, allowing the air to escape out of your upper lungs, then mildly push the remaining air out of your lower lungs. Last time, breath in through your nose filling the lower and then upper lobes of your lungs to capacity. After a brief pause, slowly exhale, allowing the air to escape out of your upper lungs, then mildly push the remaining air out of your lower lungs.

Return to your natural breathing pattern and begin to visualize the Root Chakra, swirling below the trunk of the body, before it attaches to the base of your spine. The Root Chakra is associated with the element earth, the color red, and the scent of cinnamon. Visualize yourself in nature on the last warm day of fall, toes buried in the soil and surrounded by vivid red leaves while drinking warm apple cider spiced with cinnamon. As you breathe, the

Root Chakra opens, allowing an increase of SoZoKi to enter your ethereal body. The Root is the chakra of inspiration, and as inspired thought enters your conscious mind through the root, it feeds the remaining chakras located within your ethereal body.

Continue breathing, in through your nose and out through your mouth. Visualize the minor chakras in your feet opening, allowing your energy to flow across the earth, slightly entering the soil. Bring to your mind's eye a beautiful, lush weeping willow tree. Ground your spirit energy, as roots of the willow, just below the surface. Lightly attach your spirit to earth before sending it up and out to all of creation, past the clear blue sky, moving through the stars of the Milky Way, beyond this universe and into all that is exists. Request SoZoKi to enter your ethereal body through the Root and minor chakras of your hands while your feet chakras keep your spirit grounded to earth.

Continue breathing and bring your focus up to the Sacral Chakra, located just below your navel, guiding SoZoKi up from the Root and into this chakra. The sacral chakra is associated with the element water, the color orange, and the scent of dragon's blood. Orange symbolizes energy, excitement, vitality, and good health. Sacral is the chakra of intuition of the inspired thought that entered through the Root. Still in nature during the fall season, visualize yourself sitting on a rock with your feet in a pool of water. As you continue to breathe, light a dragon's blood incense stick, filling your being with the scent as you are drenched in the color of orange leaves dancing in the breeze of a cool fall day.

As SoZoKi is pulled upward to enter the Solar Plexus, acknowledge the inspired thought that entered through the Root and was intuited in the Sacral chakras, entering the Solar Plexus for an opinion or judgement to be formed. The element associated with this chakra is fire, the color is yellow, and the scent is ginger. Continue to visualize yourself in nature, sitting by a fire, and as the yellow flames dance, breathe in the scent of ginger from the plants that surround you.

As you visualize SoZoKi being pushed from the Solar Plexus up and into your Heart Chakra located in the middle of your breastbone continue to allow your natural breathing pattern. Envision SoZoKi carrying the opinion or judgement formed in the Solar Plexus into your heart chakra and seize the opportunity to re-consider if needed. The element associated with the Heart Chakra is air, the color is green, and the scent is rose. Remaining in nature visualize yourself walking into a rose garden as your bare feet sink into a lush green lawn. Breath in the fresh air to smell the sweet scent of the roses as you focus on re-consideration of judgments and opinions.

As SoZoKi continues its upward movement it is

pushed from the Heart and pulled into the Throat, the chakra of communication. Inspired thought has been intuited and judged in the lower chakras, moved into the upper heart chakra where it has been reconsidered before it enters the Throat where it is vocalized to the world. The element associated with the Throat Chakra is ether, the clear sky, the heavens. The color associated with this chakra is blue, and the scent is sandalwood. Visualize yourself walking out of the rose garden and into a lush green field. As you lay down in the field, your eyes are drenched in the color of a clear blue sky while you breathe in the scent of sandalwood. Continue to breathe in through your nose, and then gently releasing your breath out of your mouth.

In its ever upward movement, SoZoKi is pulled out of the throat and into the Third Eye Chakra, the chakra of understanding your place in creation. With SoZoKi you have experienced inspired thought, intuited then formed an opinion or made a judgement, and reconsidered before vocalizing to the world. As SoZoKi enters the Third Eye you see yourself as a part of, rather than separate from, all that exists. Not above, not below, but in perfect unison with creation, giving you the clairvoyant ability to see with this chakra what you cannot with eyes. The element associated with the Third Eye is light, the color is indigo, and the scent is lavender. After soaking up the blue sky, visualize yourself leaving the green field as you enter a new one abundant with lavender and wild indigo flowers. As you stand in the field sunshine falls gently upon your head while you are surrounded with the color indigo as you breathe in the sweet floral scent of lavender that fills the air. Continue your natural breathing pattern, in through your nose and then gently escaping out of your mouth.

From the Third Eye, SoZoKi leaves the body, moving upward to enter the Crown, the chakra of enlightenment. Having confirmed your place in creation, you now connect to the Divine, Holy Spirit to Holy Spirit, allowing SoZoKi to exit your ethereal body, return to creation and then re-enter though the root in the eternal communion of human and spiritual consciousness. The element associated with the Crown Chakra is thought. Attaching your Holy Spirit to God Spirit, your thoughts are drenched in white or violet light as you continue your walk and arrive in a field of wild jasmine. Once released from the Crown, SoZoKi enters the Root sustaining a continuous flow to fill, sustain, inspire, and guide your consciousness, attaching human to spirit.

When you are ready bring your spirit fully back into your human consciousness. Wiggle your fingers and toes. Take a deep breath in through your nose then allow it to move out of your lungs through your mouth. Slowly open your eyes. Take this moment to reflect on yourself, the experience of

communing with the Divine through the help of
SoZoKi and give thanks for the opportunity to have
lifted your spirit with Creation and The Creator.

Consider finishing your mediation with this mantra:

Allow creation's energy to manifest and
sustain light, love and truth in my life,
today and every day.

Epilogue

The thirty-minute drive between Carmel and Salinas gives me an hour each day to stream thoughts into a meaningful conversation with myself and any higher beings that may care to listen in. "The silent speech of thought" is a line I have had for decades, knowing it would find its home in a future poetic inspiration. And now I find it fitting in this book at this time. It defines the internal process of conversation with self, with Spirit, with God, carrying the speaker beyond ritual repetitions into possibility; potential...there are no limits.

The journey for this book – I specifically chose these particular words for the book has taken on its own life – has been filled with pushing and frequent prodding in a clear attempt to get me to deliver. An incessant thought has been that the portrait of the soul can only be painted with words, and it has drifted through my mind as I drove through the agriculture fields of the central California coast. It is my sincere hope that my words have given you the tools to paint your own soul's portrait.

The Reiki Master Degree certification identifies the practitioner as an attuned teacher. When I earned the certification, in December of 1999, my master teacher shared she thought I would change the practice and name. At the time I did not think twice about what she shared, and it was ten years before I had any desire to begin writing on the subject of interjecting Reiki into the nursing process.

The first inception of this book was in 2009, and its purpose was to teach nurses to incorporate Reiki into their health care process. That evolved into the creation of the word *SoZoKi* to define a practice *Ésprit with SoZoKi*, taking energy practice out of the hands of a practitioner and make it your own... literally!

Earlier I shared details of the summer of 2018 in Charlottesville when I started with one book idea and it transformed into this one. As my writing was ending, my day job work picked up, and I moved to Miami as a travel leader in the operating rooms at Jackson Memorial Hospital.

While I worked on my career, I began the Trademark application process for the word SoZoKi and worked on art while my friend, Annie, began editing my book when her own work/life allowed. In May of 2019, my contract ended in Miami and I accepted a contract offer in a small desert town in California, identified as a Critical Access Hospital. (A CAH has a maximum of 25 beds and is located in a rural area more than over 35 miles from another hospital, or that is 15 miles from another hospital but in mountainous terrain accessible only by only secondary roads.) After only a month, I notified the hospital and the travel nurse company that I was immediately ending the contract, due to unsafe practices and environments that were not going to change.

There I was again...out of work, time on my hands, and driving back across the country to regroup. During that ride came the inspiration to partition the book to create a manual for nursing continuing education. Instead of teaching the nurse to incorporate Reiki into their practice, I would teach the nurse to bring SoZoKi into their personal life for themselves.

I submitted the course to present at the AORN International Expo as a Poster Presentation. As I had been advancing my nursing leadership path and wanted to continue on that trajectory, I had to be talked into accepting an education contract. Work is work and the contract was less demanding, so I accepted and headed back across country. Did I mention that by this point, I was in Miami, had gone to Virginia, then California, back to Virginia, and now it meant heading back to the Left Coast? Whew!

So I was just out here on the California Central Coast with a contract, and I got an offer for the permanent position. But not as an educator. On day three out here, I was asked to take on the director role while keeping the educator role! So much for a less demanding job.

Finding a place to live in Monterey County is next to impossible, but I received a surprise call from a realtor who offered me a wonderful apartment in Carmel. Most importantly, my little dogs were welcome!

Then, as luck would have it – or as synchronicity continued on this exceptional journey – I met my neighbor, a wonderful man named Gerard Rose, who happens to be an author and who agreed to read my manuscript. He in turn agreed to share my manuscript with his publisher...who is now my publisher.

Now I find myself finishing my book, reflecting on how it all came to be.

About the Author

Nancy Anna Blitz is the birth and artistic name used by the author. It is as well her legal name when her first nursing degree, Associate Degree in Nursing (ADN), was earned at a community college in Southeast Alabama, and when she was awarded "Who's Who in American Junior Colleges."

The name Nancy Blitz Ruff is the author's professional name under which she advanced her education. First acquiring formal recognition for reaching the Reiki I and II practitioner levels, before earning the Reiki Master Degree (a certification, not an academic degree), and then spending two years reviewing the literature, balancing Western evidence-based rationale with Eastern esoteric cultural practices.

Nancy worked in a collaborative university setting with a variety of chronic pain and chronic/acute anxiety patients, before returning to Western academia. She earned a Bachelor's and then Master's Degree of Science in Nursing at Western Governor's University while filling the role of an evening charge RN at the University of Virginia.

Nancy has held certification (CNOR) in her specialty of surgical services, has been accepted to present at the Association of periOperative Registered Nurses (AORN) International Expo, and has written a continuing education (CE) course to assist in preventing provider burnout. Her work has taken Nancy to 23 hospitals across the United States and Hawaii. From a small rural two-room hospital to multiple large tertiary care Level I Trauma Teaching University hospitals in L.A., New Orleans, Washington D.C., Charlottesville, Virginia, and Miami, Nancy has spent 38 years observing humanity in a most vulnerable state while providing care for and comfort to both patients and colleagues. At the time of the initial publication of this book, she held the Perioperative Services Directorship, leading seven units and 120 employees who provide surgical services to the people of the Salinas Valley of California.

Key players in her journey were her mother, Jenelle Malloy Blitz, an RN; her father Navy Lieutenant Commander Victor Edward Blitz, Sr.; her ex-husband, Dr. Mark Mosley Ruff; and still today, her son, Tyler Mosley Blitz Ruff.

SETON
PUBLISHING

Made in the USA
Middletown, DE
16 June 2021

41443029R00116